Write a

Will

The Fastest and Easiest Guide to Write Your Own Will

(Last Will and Testament, Estate Planning, Legal Briefs, Emanuel Law Outlines, Understanding)

Kevin Daniels

Published By **Chris David**

Kevin Daniels

Write a Will: The Fastest and Easiest Guide to Write Your Own Will (Last Will and Testament, Estate Planning, Legal Briefs, Emanuel Law Outlines, Understanding)

ISBN 978-1-998038-94-7

No part of this guidebook shall be reproduced in any form without permission in writing from the publisher except in the case of brief quotations embodied in critical articles or reviews.

Legal & Disclaimer

The information contained in this book is not designed to replace or take the place of any form of medicine or professional medical advice. The information in this book has been provided for educational & entertainment purposes only.

The information contained in this book has been compiled from sources deemed reliable, and it is accurate to the best of the Author's knowledge; however, the Author cannot guarantee its accuracy and validity and cannot be held liable for any errors or omissions. Changes are periodically made to this book. You must consult your doctor or get professional medical advice before using any of the suggested remedies, techniques, or information in this book.

Table Of Contents

Chapter 1: Who ought to make a will?

An individual making a will is called a testator. There are fundamental requirements that sdetermine who may additionally need to make a valid will. The first is age and the second one is functionality.

In most global places you must first attain the age of majority earlier than you can make your private will. In present day, it's far each sixteen, 18 or 21 years old. The handiest exception in a few nations is a minor who is getting married, is married, or whose marriage has ended. In all special instances, if a minor wants to have a valid will, normally in situations wherein they already have a enormous assets, maximum nations provide a criminal process known as a statutory will application. This is in which the criminal guardian of the minor will make an software to the court docket to make a will on behalf of the minor.

When it includes ability, or extra specially testamentary capability, I can verify from revel in that this is one of the maximum litigious troubles in succession regulation.

In famous, testamentary capability requires the subsequent: whilst you made and finished your will you had been of sound mind and memory, you knew what you were doing, you understood the prison way of making a will and also you likely did so freely and voluntarily, without any undue effect or duress, after evaluating the extent of your own home and all the possible beneficiaries that might have a legitimate expectation to be named on your will.

When you have interaction the services of a expert will drafter for your usa, whether or no longer or now not it is an legal professional, solicitor, or notary, it is going to be one in every of his or her duties to meet themselves which you do in reality non-public the important testamentary capacity in advance than they assist you in making and executing your will. As stated below, their proof to the court might be extensively probative inside the event of a task to your testamentary capability.

In most times in that you have had been given a will this is valid at the face of it, that means that it became properly drafted and completed (signed efficiently through you and your witnesses), the courts will presume that the testator did in reality have testamentary capacity on the identical time as it grow to be finished. It is then for the individual that avers that the testator did now not have or could not have had testamentary capability when the desire come to be completed, to vicinity sufficient proof earlier than the courtroom to disprove testamentary functionality. As you could recollect, this isn't an clean burden of proof. The courts do no longer care about your opinions or suspicions until you can lower back it up with sufficient authentic proof to influence the courtroom in any other case on a stability of possibilities. This shape of proof is commonly inside the shape of expert clinical critiques as to the testamentary capability of the testator at the time of execution of the need. If your will become professionally drafted, the preference drafter's evidence in this regard might be quite probative, mainly if the need drafter has hundreds of years of experience in the concern.

If an character character loses his or her testamentary capacity, they can't make or execute a legitimate will. In such a case, similar to with minors, their jail mum or dad want to technique the courtroom docket docket to make a statutory will on their behalf.

ooOoo

Returned to top

Returned to Table of Contents

Chapter 2: Requirements for a valid will

There are appreciably speaking handiest 5 requirements for a legitimate will which is probably implemented in maximum worldwide locations. First, there have to be a report. Second, the report need to be in writing. Third, the document needs to consist of the testamentary intentions of the character making the selection (the testator). Fourth, the file want to be signed through the usage of the testator on the quit thereof with the motive that the record will thereby perform as his or her final will and testomony. Fifth, the signature of the testator need to be properly witnessed with the useful resource of capable witnesses.

A easy Google trying to find to your u . S . Will confirm whether or not your u . S . A . Has more or particular necessities for a valid will.

A will that complies with these 5 requirements will on the face of or not it's declared a legitimate will of the preference maker and will stay on most, if no longer all, disturbing situations.

Now allow's test the ones requirements for my part to make clear them and to make sure that you apprehend them efficaciously.

A file

This requirement sounds simple sufficient if by manner of record you recognize it to be a piece of paper or quantities of paper joined collectively. The common definition of a file is a written or found out paper presenting statistics or proof. This definition has been widened thru the courts with reference to casual will programs to consist of laptop documents, video documents, textual content messages and so on, within the essential due to the reality those might be transcribed or located out out in file form. To show those extraordinary media paperwork in court docket docket, which aren't yet in document form, is an costly technique. If you typed and saved your will in a computer report, you may glaringly want to print it out in advance than you and your witnesses signal it.

In writing

The trendy traditional kinds of writing are handwritten documents and typewritten files.

However, in some worldwide places together with France, in case you need to jot down down your private will, it ought to be for your very very own handwriting. In the occasion of a hassle, this will allow a handwriting professional to verify that it emerge as certainly your personal handwriting.

Additionally, if the need is on your very very own handwriting, it's also an example that what is written is indeed your testamentary intentions and no longer the ones of someone else, and which you knew and authorized the contents thereof.

Testamentary intentions

The primary motive of your will is to tell your executor how and to whom your assets want to be allotted. This is called your testamentary intentions. You ought to apprehend and approve of all your testamentary intentions in advance than you signal your will.

Do not write some thing else to your will. Your will need to consist of best your testamentary intentions and no longer some thing greater. Your will isn't the appropriate place to air your grimy laundry, nor to slander, disgrace, or rebuke all and sundry. If you do want to head away a selected message to a particular person, achieve this in a separate document that isn't always your will. If you located beside the point, slanderous, vexatious, or scandalous cloth on your will, a court docket software can be needed to dispose of it before probate of your will can be ordered. You moreover run the danger that your will might be declared invalid. And positive, your own home will need to bear the costs of this sort of software program, so don't do it.

Signed thru the testator

The cause of your signature is to signify that you understand and approve of the contents of your will, and also you need this document to be your closing will and testomony.

If the need is to your very very own handwriting, the presumption is probably that you knew and licensed of its contents in advance than you finished it. If, but, it's far a typewritten will and you in all likelihood did now not type it yourself, you need to examine it, or have it study to you, earlier than you signal it. This is in particular essential in which you knowledgeable a person else, like a professional will drafter, to draft your will. The reason you must have a look at over it first is to meet yourself that the preference does now not contain any mistakes and that the desire drafter has really positioned your testamentary intentions into the need as you wanted them. If there are any terms or terms in your will that confuse you or which you do not recognize, ask the want drafter for clarification and to give an reason behind them to you.

Some expert will drafters will observe the need once more to you, and within the gadget offer an purpose for any crook phrases or clauses which you might be unsure of or do not recognize, to meet themselves that you apprehend and approve of the contents of the need.

Do not ask considered actually one in every of your intended beneficiaries to draft your will to your behalf besides it is your simplest preference. It isn't a jail requirement that they don't, however it creates what is called a suspicious situation. It might likely provide upward push to investigations once you surpassed away into whether or not or now not your will must be contested. You do not want any suspicions approximately undue impact or duress to be attached on your will, and it's miles better to keep away from it as high-quality as you could.

Where on the record must you sign your will? Some global locations require you to sign at the bottom of each internet net web page of the desire in addition to at the end of your will. This is proper workout. The prevent of your will is not on the lowest of the final web page, however right after the closing paragraph of your will. Other international locations only require you to sign the choice on the forestall thereof and not each internet web page. However, it is ideal exercise to sign at the lowest of every web web page as properly, no matter the truth that it isn't always a criminal requirement on your u . S . A ., because it prevents humans from setting or getting rid of pages afterwards.

A whole signature is needed, but if the testator can pleasant make a mark with the goal for it to be his or her signature, that might be prison too.

If the testator can't sign in any respect, he can teach someone else to join up his behalf, however most effective if that individual does so in his presence. In the form of case, that man or woman ought to no longer be a beneficiary.

An example of a signature clause for the want maker at the prevent of his or her will is as follows:

Signed with the aid of me in this ….. Day of ………….2021. (insert day and month) within the presence of the two witnesses who shall attest to this, my signature.

_____

(be a part of up the street)

Signature of (insert complete names of the testator)

Testator's signature have to be witnessed

Most global places require the presence of two witnesses at the identical time as the desire maker symptoms and signs and signs and symptoms his or her will. The cause of the witnesses is to affirm and affirm that it became truly the testator who signed the need, as they saw it with their very personal eyes. They need not apprehend what is in the will and want not be gift while the preference is have a take a look at and explained to the selection maker, but they want to be present whilst the choice maker signs and signs the will.

Although a few international places allow a beneficiary under the choice to be a witness to in an effort to, maximum worldwide locations do no longer. Therefore, do not ask considered without a doubt certainly one of your beneficiaries to behave as a witness, as it'd disqualify them from taking a advantage from your will.

A critical element of signing and witnessing the signature of the testator is that each one 3 events, the testator and the 2 witnesses, need to be in each unique's presence concurrently after they signal. In exclusive phrases, every witnesses look on on the same time as the testator signs and symptoms and signs the selection. Thereafter, the number one witness symptoms the selection as a witness, whilst the testator and the second witness appearance on. Then the second witness symptoms the need, on the same time because the number one witness and the testator look on. Only then can or now not it's stated that your turns into validly completed.

Although it's also not a criminal requirement that your will have to be dated, it's far prudent to perform that. This turns into quite relevant if after your loss of life there's multiple will that purports to be your ultimate will and testament, in particular in the occasion that they every include revocation clauses, and the court need to determine which became in fact your last will.

Good workout should therefore be for the testator to sign each web page of his will at the lowest thereof and the final net internet page on the surrender thereof after which for the witnesses to do the identical. If your will is typewritten, you may make a provision in the footer of every internet page for "Witness 1", "Witness 2" and "Testator" and a area for each to sign. At the save you of your will, you may have a testator's signature clause containing the region and date of signature and an attestation clause in your witnesses.

In maximum countries, a validly achieved will gives upward push to the following legal presumptions:

*That the want has been well performed.

*That the testator changed into of sound mind and reminiscence on the same time as the desire turn out to be finished.

*That the testator had testamentary capability whilst the selection grow to be done.

*That the testator knew and widespread of the contents of the choice.

Like all different prison presumptions, those presumptions can be rebutted, however it's going to require enough relevant proof to perform that. As stated earlier than, the crook burden of proof to influence a court docket docket docket of law in any other case is not an clean one. Your suspicions and circumstantial proof want to be backed up with hard evidence in advance than the court docket will rebut these presumptions. It is exceptionally advocated which you get impartial crook advice earlier than you contest a will that is well executed.

In the following bankruptcy we are able to have a look at a few essential clauses on your will. One such clause is the attestation clause which applies to the signing and witnessing of your will.

Here is an instance of such an attestation clause:

We hereby attest that we witnessed the testator signal this can and testament in our presence at the same time as each people have been present. We are also signing as witnesses in each different's presence, in addition to inside the presence of the testator.

_____

Signature of witness 1

(Full name of witness 1)

(Address of witness 1)

_____

Signature of witness 2

(Full name of witness 2)

(Address of witness 2)

Failure to conform with those prison requirements

As said earlier than, a failure to comply with one or greater of those felony requirements will depart you with an informal will at remarkable. Sadly, some international places are lagging of their legal reform and do no longer understand the possibility of an casual will and will virtually declare which you died intestate, i.E., with out a legitimate will.

In different countries in that permits you to reform has already taken vicinity, like Australia and the United Kingdom, your will can nevertheless be stored if it does not look at all the crook necessities if the courtroom docket is satisfied that there may be in truth a report that includes the testamentary intentions of the deceased, and that he or she supposed that report to be his or her ultimate will and testament.

For instance, some courts have allowed video wills, audio wills, textual content message wills and voice message wills to be the final will and testament of the deceased. However, the court docket packages to have those informal wills declared to be the ultimate will and testomony of the deceased are extremely luxurious, despite the fact that they may be uncontested, due to the fact they require a number of expert proof. If they'll be contested, even greater so. Avoid the ones situations at all charges. It is straightforward enough to create and execute your very own valid will if you be aware of and follow the felony necessities relevant for your united states of america of america.

Chapter 3: Essential clauses

Next, we're going to speak approximately a few crucial clauses that have to be on your will. These aren't prison requirements, however they will be clauses that serve real capabilities.

Commencement clause

It isn't always vital to have a name net web page for your will, despite the fact that maximum perceive pages simply usa:

The Last Will and Testament of (full call of testator)

That said, the commencement clause of your will is vital due to the reality this tells the area the reason of your report. A lot of human beings have testamentary writings which are not supposed to be their will however are in simple phrases a technique for them to type out their thoughts and make up their minds as to how and to whom they want to distribute their belongings. The commencement clause of your will want to therefore u . S . Your real purpose of this record to be your very last will and testament.

A useful precedent for this sort of clause is as follows:

I, (insert testator's complete name and surname) of (insert your current-day residential address, together with nation and u . S . A .) declare this to be my Last Will and Testament.

This is normally accompanied through a revocation clause.

Revocation clause

Whenever you are making a latest will, you generally want this can to replace any previous wills that you may have executed. This need to be done expressly, in any other case you can take a seat with a couple of valid will and the courts will attempt to offer impact to the ones styles of wills as a ways as feasible. This is obviously no longer what you need. A clean revocation clause in the beginning of your will solves this trouble. A useful precedent for this kind of clause is as follows:

I hereby revoke all previous wills, codicils and or testamentary writings that I may also have made and claim this to be my final will and testament.

The only time you need to leave a couple of legitimate will is if you have property in high-quality international locations.

These days, it is not unusual for will makers to have estates comprising of belongings which may be in amazing worldwide locations. Although you could cope with those varieties of belongings in one single will, it is not honestly beneficial an excellent manner to achieve this for the smooth motive that your executor will run into practical problems seeking to transfer property which can be in awesome global locations. The transfer of those property typically calls for the presence and production of the specific will, as a way to be complicated due to the reality there can handiest be one unique will and every countries can't have it concurrently. This will cause vain delays and incur more charges if you need to need to be paid out of your property.

Therefore, when you have belongings in extraordinary global places, it is beneficial to have a separate will for each of your estates in those nations.

If for instance you have got got assets in each Australia and England, a beneficial precedent to your graduation and revocation clauses in the sort of case is as follows:

I, (insert testator's complete name and surname) of (insert your present day residential address, which includes us of a and u . S .) claim this to be my Last Will and Testament referring to my (insert america, e.G., "Australian") estate handiest.

I hereby revoke all preceding wills, codicils and or testamentary writings that I might also moreover additionally have made concerning my (insert usa, e.G., "Australian") assets and claim this to be my remaining will and testament for my (insert u . S ., e.G., "Australian") assets.

Any belongings that shape a part of my property in (insert unique u . S . A ., e.G., "England") need to be allotted according with my (insert tremendous usa of the united states, e.G., "English") will.

This very last sentence isn't technically vital, but it signs the reader of your will of the existence of a separate will pertaining to your English property, in addition to the life of property you would possibly have in England. This will positioned them on alert to look for this shape of will. It is in reality beneficial to hold all of your wills together in a single place and inform your executor wherein he or she will be able to discover them after your death. Most expert will drafters will provide to hold your completed will secure till it is desired. In that case, you ought to though inform your executor or beneficiaries wherein your will or wills may be located even as you surpassed away.

If you've got separate wills to your estates in precise nations, it is very essential that you maintain the contents of each will separate. Do no longer as an example test along with your English assets for your Australian will and vice versa. If you have got have been given a country unique will, the purpose of on the manner to is to distribute your own home in that unique the united states, and not some thing else.

If for instance you have were given a guardianship clause on your Australian will that offers with the guardianship of your minor youngsters, you can not in truth have a guardianship clause in your English will, as an awesome way to create a warfare. Your guardianship and burial wishes clauses must be contained in the will in which you have your permanent residency. The different wills need to simplest address assets which you have in the ones international locations.

If you quality have belongings in a single u . S ., you don't have to worry about the above. In that case it isn't crucial at the way to specify your home via usa of the us of the united states and your will's graduation and revocation clauses should then without a doubt check:

I, (insert testator's entire call and surname) of (insert your current-day residential address, including kingdom and u.S. Of the usa) claim this to be my Last Will and Testament.

I hereby revoke all previous wills, codicils and or testamentary writings that I may additionally have made and claim this to be my remaining will and testomony.

Appointing your executor

The next component you need to do is to hire an executor for your property. This is the depended on individual that allows you to be tasked with the execution of your testamentary wishes. He or she will be able to follow for probate of your estate, whereafter they may maintain with the administration and distribution thereof. They will generally moreover be the accountable person making all your funeral preparations.

In exercise, your executor will typically teach an belongings legal expert to attend to the management of the property on their behalf. This makes revel in, because the belongings prison professionals understand the approach lower again to the front and function all the systems in place to administrate your own home as successfully as possible.

In a few international places you may employ more than one executor for your property, however this is not encouraged as disagreements amongst executors commonly cause delays and frustration at a few level inside the manage and distribution machine. If you've got a relied on attorney that you can hire as executor, or co-executor, it may assist speed up the manner. The better way to do it is to lease possibility executors. This manner you make certain that in case your first-preference executor cannot or does not need to without a doubt receive their appointment as such, there can be an opportunity person nominated to accomplish that.

If you fail to appoint an executor, or in case your named executor does not gather their appointment, the court will rent an executor in your own home.

During the management manner, your executor gets higher all wonderful monies because of your home, pay any high-quality money owed you may have, and hold to distribute the rest of your estate according along with your testamentary desires.

It is not unusual for testators to hire one or more in their beneficiaries to be the executor of the assets, mainly inside the event that they most effective have one beneficiary or one crucial beneficiary. They are usually encouraged to get the procedure completed as expeditiously as possible.

However, in a few conditions, it is able to be complicated for a beneficiary to also be the executor of the belongings, mainly in occasions where there may be warfare many of the particular beneficiaries, or if the named executor has a struggle of hobby as executor of the estate in preference to their interest as a beneficiary. If that is the case, they need to continuously positioned the assets's interest above their very private personal interest as a beneficiary.

For example, the spouse of the deceased is the nominated executor in addition to one of the named beneficiaries in the will. If the deceased left a life coverage coverage with out a legitimate nominees, the insurance agency normally has a discretion to whom the proceeds of the insurance need to be paid. If the executor of the assets applies for the proceeds to be paid to her in her private potential and no longer to the property, she is putting her interests above those of the estate. This she can't do.

It is important as a way to understand that the proceeds of existence insurance guidelines do no longer typically shape part of your estate property. You can't therefore depart or gift the proceeds of your life coverage policies to a particular beneficiary in your will. The correct way to do this is to appoint a beneficiary underneath your insurance. Those nominations normally expire after a three hundred and sixty 5 days or and ought to be renewed thru you to live valid. Most life coverage tips reserve a discretion within the trustee of the coverage as to whom the proceeds need to be paid to. If you are unsure about any modern-day nominees below your existence coverage rules, you want to conform with this up together together with your supplier or the relevant insurance organisation as a depend of urgency.

A precedent for the appointment of a unmarried executor is as follows:

I hereby hire my wife (insert full call of wife) to be the executor of my will.

A precedent for the appointment of an opportunity executor is as follows:

I hereby employ my spouse (insert full name of spouse) to be the executor of my will. If for a few reason she isn't always able or unwilling to act as such, I hire my son (insert full name of son) as executor.

Distribution clauses

The distribution clauses are thru a long manner the maximum essential clauses to your will as they inform your executor who receives what.

This is some other area of will making that frequently ends in crook courtroom instances, commonly within the shape of packages for rectification of the choice or to get clarification or tips from the court docket docket as to how a high quality distribution clause want to be interpreted. The ordinary offender: an ambiguous testamentary motive.

When it comes to will writing, specially your distribution clauses, you want to take care to talk your intentions on this form of way that there can be amazing one feasible interpretation.

It is vital which you articulate your testamentary intentions as genuinely as viable. Do no longer attempt to use 'legalese' or phrases you do no longer recognise the general that means of. Your intention is to virtually and concisely nation who gets what. If the provisions of your will are indistinct or can also want to have multiple which means, and in case your testamentary intentions are not crystal clean, your executor will want to deliver a court software to get explanation or a path as to how a high quality clause ought to be interpreted. And positive, those packages are expensive, and people prices are typically deducted from your own home as you have got been the motive of those court cases due to the fact you had been doubtful or sloppy on your will writing.

Examples:

Gifting the identical asset instances

When you deliver a tremendous asset to a positive beneficiary, you can't deal with that asset again later on your will. This will create confusion and uncertainty.

Misdescription of an asset or a beneficiary

I provide my farm, Blackberry, to my son John Benson. (The farm's call is Blackmerry or the son's name is in truth Johan Benson but were given misspelled with the useful resource of the use of the desire drafter.)

Not describing your beneficiaries well

I offer my piano to my preferred daughter. (If you have got more than one daughter, which daughter are you speaking approximately?)

Failing to offer for contingencies

I supply my property to my 4 kids, John, Mary, Ben and Clarice in same stocks. (If one or extra of your children die in advance than you, who is supposed to get that percent? Is it their children, or must that proportion be allocated among the genuine beneficiaries, or want to that percent fall into the residue part of your private home?)

It is important that you realise and admire the entire amount of your home, in addition to maintain in mind all the people that might have a legitimate expectation to be named as a beneficiary underneath your will in advance than you decide who gets what. Remember, you could excellent supply what's lawfully yours. You can not bequeath a few component to your will that belongs to someone else, or it is co-owned by someone else. In the latter case, you may extremely good bequeath your percentage in that particular asset.

Survivorship clauses

You must moreover consider what ought to display up if the man or woman you want to benefit below your will predeceases you, dies on the same day as you, or dies inside 30 days of you. These are known as survivorship clauses. The 30-day survivorship length has been legislated for in a few international locations.

Practically it comes all the manner proper down to considering feasible eventualities. For instance, if you need to move away your complete assets on your wife but she predeceases you or dies inner 30 days of you, you want your entire property to go to your kids in same stocks. In that case you may in reality country:

I deliver my entire assets virtually to my spouse (insert full name of spouse). In the occasion that my companion predeceases me, or dies inner 30 days of me, I offer my whole estate without a doubt to my 3 youngsters (complete name of first little one), (entire name of 2nd child) and (complete name of 1/three toddler) in identical stocks.

What if one in every of your above-noted youngsters predeceases you? What have to then rise up to that predeceased toddler's percentage? If your purpose is only to advantage your kids and no longer any of your grandchildren, you need to make that smooth. For example:

I deliver my whole belongings simply to my wife (insert entire call of partner). In the occasion that my wife predeceases me, or dies inside 30 days of me, I give my entire property actually to my surviving youngsters in identical shares.

In this case the best query can be "Who had been your surviving children?"

If however you need the predeceased toddler's percent to visit his or her youngsters, you've got to say that. For example:

I deliver my whole assets truely to my spouse (insert full name of wife). In the occasion that my spouse predeceases me, or dies internal 30 days of me, I offer my entire property simply to my three children (whole name of first toddler), (full name of 2nd infant) and (full name of one/three infant) in identical shares. If any of my kids predeceases me, I offer their percent to their kids in same shares.

On the difficulty of children, it should be said that, in maximum global locations, observed children are through the usage of law seemed as the children of the determined dad and mom and no longer the children of the natural dad and mom. Therefore, when you have a herbal infant that changed into located out if you have been more youthful, and after which you had more organic children, the child that have come to be adopted out is now not via law your toddler. If for your will you are making a bequest to your "youngsters", your toddler that was accompanied out will no longer inherit from you, as they're not covered in that description. If you need that child to inherit, you ought to especially say so.

Alternative devices or now not

You want to additionally don't forget what you would really like to appear if the element you need to provide underneath your will not exists or isn't always owned through you at the date of your death. Would you need that specific beneficiary to get keep of an opportunity gift, or do you genuinely want the existing to lapse?

There are one-of-a-kind strategies in which you may distribute your house. You can for instance make specific objects to unique human beings. These are referred to as legacies. Here are a few examples:

I provide my gold Cartier watch and matching gold Cartier earrings to my daughter (insert entire name of daughter). If my stated daughter predeceases me or dies within 30 days of me, or if I no longer non-public this watch and jewellery on the time of my death, this present shall lapse.

I deliver my gold Cartier watch and matching gold Cartier rings to my daughter (insert complete call of daughter). If my stated daughter predeceases me or dies inner 30 days of me, I gift this watch and jewelry to her daughter, my granddaughter (insert full call of the granddaughter). If I now not personal this watch and jewelry at the time of my loss of existence, this present shall lapse.

I offer my 1962 Corvette to my son (insert entire name of son). If I not very very own this car on the date of my loss of lifestyles, this present need to be replaced with a present of $25,000 to him. If my stated son predeceases me or dies interior 30 days of me, this gift, as well as the artificial present, shall lapse.

I deliver $10,000 (ten thousand greenbacks) to my excellent pal (insert name of great friend in addition to his or her final identified cope with).

I supply the family farm known as (insert name and deal with of the farm) to my son (insert whole call of son).

I supply $5,000 (5 thousand dollars) each to the following charities: the (call and cope with of the primary charity) and (call and deal with of 2d charity).

You can also make gives to a category of humans, as an instance your kids, grandchildren, nephews, nieces and so forth. For instance:

I supply $1,000 to each of my grandchildren who stay to inform the tale me.

I supply the residue of my assets to my grandchildren who stay on me in equal shares.

Guardianship clause

If you have were given minor youngsters, and inside the event that each you and your spouse die concurrently or internal 30 days of each different, you'll want someone of your choosing to look after them and lift them until they benefit the age of majority.

It is essential to canvas those possible conditions with your proposed guardians and get their permission to be named as such for your will. This will prevent a scenario in which guardianship is sprung upon them, and the opportunity of them refusing the appointment, leaving your minor youngsters with out a jail parent. It may also make clean the problem for other family who may in any other case need to behave as guardians to your children.

An instance of a guardianship clause regarding 3 minor youngsters is as follows:

In the event that my accomplice and I die concurrently or inside 30 days of every exclusive, I hire (entire names and address of proposed guardians) as guardians of my minor youngsters (entire name of child), (full name of toddler), and (entire call of infant). In the event that my proposed guardians are for in besides cause no longer able to behave as guardians, or do now not get keep of this appointment, I appoint (full names and deal with) as alternative guardians.

Testamentary trusts

A testamentary bear in mind clause isn't an important clause for your will. However, a variety of humans choose to use testamentary trusts as a vehicle to maintain their minor youngsters's inheritance secure until they achieve a sure age. A testamentary accept as real with is a agree with which you create to your will. Because your will simplest becomes operative even as you skip away, the testamentary don't forget is also satisfactory created after your loss of existence. The use of testamentary trusts is well-known in quite some international locations. However, not all countries understand trusts. If you're thinking about the use of a testamentary accept as authentic with, it's far vital which you first confirm whether or not or now not or now not trusts are identified for your u . S ..

As a part of their property planning, some people opt to create inter vivos trusts. These are trusts which might be created on the identical time as you're although alive. These trusts also can function a vehicle to limit tax and transfer responsibilities on property. Furthermore, in a few international locations like Australia, a company may additionally act as a trustee for the accept as proper with. In workout, the testator will create a circle of relatives don't forget and employ a business enterprise of which she or he or in case of a couple, each, are shareholders within the commercial enterprise organisation. They will then transfer their property assets to the remember and feature their kids and family individuals in their deciding on because of the truth the consider beneficiaries. The simplest asset that they then need to bequeath of their wills is their percentage within the trustee enterprise. It is as a substitute endorsed which you use the services of a professional property planner if you maintain in mind growing each inter vivos or testamentary trusts.

Testamentary trusts complicate the management of your property, and I would probably advise you most effective use them if virtually crucial. Also endure in thoughts instructing a professional will drafter to draft your will for you in case you want to create testamentary trusts.

A testamentary don't forget will normally be used while the testator has minor kids. Instead of leaving their estates in reality to their minor youngsters, they might as an opportunity create a testamentary be given as authentic with for the kids. A don't forget ought to continuously have a reason and in this example the reason of the testamentary believe is probably to offer for the upbringing, fitness, and schooling of your children. They may also want to create the don't forget, lease a trustee or trustees, and then deliver their estates to the keep in mind with commands to the trustees as to how the take into account belongings need to be administered. Their minor kids is probably the beneficiaries under the agree with. A very last education to the trustees ought to be to distribute the accept as true with assets to the beneficiaries when they reach a pleasing age. A remember need to have a specific termination date as trusts are not allowed to exist in perpetuity.

But what approximately the meantime? Of route, you do no longer need your youngsters to go through trouble until they reach the distribution age in the take delivery of as actual with. You would possibly therefore empower your trustees to pay for the upbringing and care of your youngsters from the agree with assets. This need to as an instance consist of month-to-month maintenance payments to the prison guardians of your minor kids, college expenses, or scientific bills. What diploma of discretion should you need your trustees to have?

The powers, rights and duties of the trustees want to be properly described in all times. This can range from full discretionary powers to specifically restrained powers. Do you, as an example, need to provide discretionary powers for your trustees, inclusive of the power to invest a few or all the accept as true with property at their discretion until such time as the distribution clauses will kick in?

Needless to say, you must have a completely excessive degree of take into account for your trustees. You need to accept as true with that they will in all instances do the right element and act within the exquisite hobbies of your minor kids in addition to the accept as true with itself, and no longer be reckless or careless with the endure in mind property.

People who create testamentary trusts will generally, however now not continuously, appoint their executor as trustee of any testamentary trusts they devise. It is often a correct concept to in no manner have less than trustees of your testamentary receive as authentic with. If one in every of them will become incapacitated or passes away, there'll although be a final trustee who can then rent a modern co-trustee and the administration of the bear in mind could likely now not be in jeopardy.

An instance of a smooth testamentary agree with clause is:

I offer my complete property without a doubt to my partner (insert complete name of wife).

If my partner predeceases me, or dies inside 30 days of me, I supply my complete property truely upon receive as actual with, The Smith Family Trust, to my trustees for the care, protection, health, and schooling of my three youngsters (whole call of first infant), (complete call of second toddler) and (entire call of 0.33 toddler).

I lease (complete name of first trustee) and (full name of 2d trustee) as trustees of the Smith Family Trust and I direct that there should usually be no lots less than trustees. The trustees shall have the power to hire new trustees even as important.

My three kids (complete name of first toddler), (full name of 2nd child) and (entire call of one/3 infant) are the simplest beneficiaries below this agree with.

The Smith Family Trust shall terminate on the identical time because the final infant attains the age of 25, at the same time because the very last agree with property and accrued earnings shall be divided further amongst my 3 stated kids. If any of my youngsters ought to die earlier than this receive as actual with entails an cease, their share should be dispensed to their kids in same stocks. If they die leaving no kids, their consider proportion have to be divided equally some of the closing maintain in thoughts beneficiaries.

My trustees shall have the subsequent powers, rights, and duties…

This is a totally simplified testamentary do not forget clause honestly to provide you a pinnacle stage view of the easy workings thereof. If you want to create testamentary trusts, it is endorsed to are seeking for the assist of a professional will drafter.

Once your children accumulate the age of majority, or such an age in which you will be snug to apprehend that they received't squander their inheritance, I ought to endorse which you replace your will to provide their shares to them definitely, in region of upon receive as proper with.

Residuary clause

You want to get rid of all of your own home on your will. If you fail to cope with a number of your home, the court docket docket will claim those assets to be disbursed on intestacy. You do not need this to reveal up.

If you surely want to benefit one person or one business organization of human beings, for example your youngsters in identical stocks, you could genuinely provide your complete assets in fact to them. If you deliver your entire estate without a doubt, there are not any remainder or residuary assets to offer. Example:

I deliver my entire property certainly to my kids (whole names of kids) in identical stocks.

Or

I deliver my whole assets without a doubt to my spouse.

However, even as you bequeath particular devices to people in your will, there will constantly be the relaxation or residuary property.

For this purpose, testators normally encompass a residuary or the relaxation clause as their remaining distribution clause in the will. For instance:

I provide the remainder of my estate in equal shares to (insert names of beneficiaries).

I offer the the relaxation of my belongings to my husband (insert name of husband).

Remember that I cautioned you above which you cannot deliver the equal asset two times, as that could create an uncertainty as to what precisely your testamentary wishes are. Do now not consequently use the phrase I provide my entire assets simply after you have got made unique gadgets to particular human beings. This creates a contradiction. Instead, you have to as a substitute say I supply the the relaxation of my assets definitely to..., or actually virtually country I offer the the rest of my property to...

Attestation clause

The cause of an attestation clause is to indicate that the need end up nicely signed and witnessed, and therefore duly finished according with the jail requirements.

This can also be the remaining clause of your will.

It is essentially just a clause declaring that the witnesses were in the presence of the testator at the same time as she or he signed their will, and an attestation that both witnesses remained in the testator's, in addition to every other's, presence when they signed as witnesses.

Although an attestation clause is not a prison requirement for a legitimate will, it's far going a protracted way in exciting the probate courts that your becomes properly accomplished.

Here is an example of a signature and attestation clause at the forestall of a will.

Signed with the aid of me in this ..... Day of ....2021 (insert day and month) inside the presence of the 2 witnesses who shall attest to this, my signature.

_____

(be a part of up the line)

Signature of Testator (insert complete call of the testator)

This becomes signed thru the stated (insert complete call of the testator) in our presence, and attested and signed with the aid of us within the presence of him/her and every exceptional.

_____

Signature of witness

(Full name of first witness)

(Address of first witness)

_____

Signature of witness

(Full name of 2d witness)

(Address of second witness)

In the following financial ruin we're capable of delve greater into the nitty gritty of wherein to start and the manner to nicely put together to draft your will. Are you geared up?

ooOoo

over again to pinnacle

once more to Table of Contents

Chapter 4: Preparing to draft your will

The information that I shared with you in the preceding chapters want to have sufficiently prepared you to draft your very non-public will. As a depend of truth, I might not be amazed if some of you have got got already prepared a quick stopgap will to be in area on the equal time as you're making ready your subsequent will.

In this economic disaster I will take you via a smooth step-with the aid of the use of manner of-step approach that you can use within the schooling section of drafting your very very own will. You will want a pen and paper. I endorse the usage of a pocket e-book so that every one your preparatory artwork may be in a single place for easy get right of entry to later whilst you in the long run draft your will.

The purpose of those physical games is to set up the quantity and nature of your property, wheresoever those assets is probably located, and to take into account all the people that could legitimately expect to be named as beneficiaries beneath your will.

Very essential: When you placed pen on paper with the subsequent sports activities, it's miles crucial that you make it clean that this record isn't always your will but in reality notes that you are making to help you in drafting your will.

Nature and quantity of your private home

List all the belongings currently for your home. If you have got assets in notable worldwide places, make separate lists for every u . S ..

At the top of your internet net web page, write:

List of assets in my property as at (insert date)

Now maintain to list your assets from most valuable to least precious. For most people, the maximum essential asset of their property might be their home and or actual assets they very own. If you co-personal actual property, e.G. Your own family domestic, with a person else, it is very vital which you understand the man or woman of your co-possession. The actual property felony suggestions in most global places will offer for a few form of co-possession in which each co-owner owns a percentage within the property. Remember, you can't gift what you do now not have. For example, a husband and accomplice co-very own their house and each one in every of them is entitled to a 50% percentage in the property. This approach, in their wills, each of them can only dispose of their 50% percentage in the belongings, and no longer of the complete assets.

Here in Australia, there are two types of co-possession of real assets. One is proudly proudly owning the property as tenants in common, which essentially way each person holds an identical percent within the belongings and that percentage will form a part of your home, like in the example above. The 2d form is co-proudly owning the belongings as joint tenants, in which the crook scenario is an lousy lot excellent. In this situation clearly every body owns one hundred% of the assets. However, if one of the joint tenants passes away, his interest inside the property is automatically, with the useful resource of law, transferred to the last joint tenants as even though he in no way owned it in any respect. This is obviously a amazing manner for a husband and spouse (couple) to co-very personal a assets with the motive that once the primary one dies, the very last partner will keep the belongings for him or herself, with out the need of highly-priced switch responsibilities. A joint tenancy may be severed and transformed to a tenancy in not unusual by using agreement or court docket order, normally if the couple divorces or separates, in which case each co-owner can also have an equal percentage within the property, in order to then shape part of their property.

When you listing your property, be as particular as possible and list and understand every property one by one: every actual belongings, each automobile, financial organization money owed, shareholdings, stocks, retirement price variety (like your Super in Australia or your 401(ok) inside the USA), treasured collections, and so on. When you come to the lowest of your listing, you'll likely need to agency matters collectively, like non-public assets, besides there's some element of real or sentimental fee which you would really like to present one at a time.

Remember that your life coverage hints aren't part of your estate assets. Only as fast due to the fact the trustee of the precise insurance business enterprise can pay out on the coverage will there be cash that might or won't form a part of your home property, counting on whether or not or no longer or no longer you named a nominee underneath your insurance. If you probably did, the coins must visit that nominee and no longer your property. If you likely did not, the trustee usually has a discretion below the insurance to pay the life coverage moneys on software to as a minimum one or extra particular humans, for instance to the partner, kids, or to the estate of the deceased.

List of potential beneficiaries

Do not call this list "list of beneficiaries", however as an opportunity "listing of feasible or capability beneficiaries". The concept right proper right here isn't always to decide who receives what, but as a substitute to decide who may additionally probable have a claim on your bounty when you passed away. It is critical which you as a minimum recall everyone on this listing, and great then make a conscious choice afterwards who you need to advantage under your will and who you do now not need to gain.

People who're no matter the fact that financially based upon you can have a valid expectancy to be named as beneficiaries below your will. As a count number of truth, most international locations have legislated for the sufficient provision of own family participants out of your house, even earlier than your private home is finalized.

Family provision applications are currently the most litigious location of succession regulation right here in Australia. Usually, the candidates are person kids who have been omitted of the need, with or without accurate purpose, who now claim to be in economic need, and that the deceased had an duty to provide for them.

Some international locations take this moral responsibility on the deceased to provide for his or her right now family participants very notably and will permit for generous contributions from your house to them. These family provision orders manifestly effect the scale of your net estate.

Start with the aid of using putting down the names of your at once own family individuals, i.E., your partner, youngsters, and grandchildren. If you're presently financially contributing to any in their renovation and help, chances are the courts will determine that you have a continuing moral obligation to reap this through way of well presenting for them on your will.

Now write down the names of numerous individuals you would really like to gain below your will and why.

Next, write down the names of capability charities you need to gain and why.

Once you apprehend the dimensions and volume of your home, further to who all the functionality beneficiaries are, you are in a function to recollect how and to whom you need to distribute your house for your will.

List of capability legacies

Above, you have got were given identified all of your present day property and all of the individuals who you want to gain, and people who would possibly have a legitimate expectation to be named as a beneficiary beneath your will.

Now, if there are any particular property which you need to move away to a particular individual, for example a own family heirloom that you need to move away in your eldest infant, listing those right proper right here.

Examples:

Grand piano – Johnny English (eldest son)

My teaspoon collection – Joan of Arc (she loves my collection and could add it to hers)

The circle of relatives domestic at forty 3 Ashford Drive, Somerset West – my associate Sarah Barkley

$5,000 to my lifelong pal Ben Kruger

$10,000 to the Bethel Church at (deal with)

The rest of your own home assets now not indexed right here will form a part of your residuary estate. Remember, in case you plan to provide for tremendous legacies, you can not afterwards offer the whole of your home to any of your beneficiaries. You can simplest supply the residuary assets.

Residuary belongings

Now it's time if you need to undergo in thoughts who you need to go away the rest of your property to, and in what stocks. These are the property that live after all of the legacies are given.

Example:

I deliver the the relaxation of my property in same shares to (insert names of beneficiaries).

Potential executors

List the people you're thinking about as executors right here.

Potential guardians

If you have were given minor youngsters, list the humans you're considering as feasible guardians for them proper here. It is higher to test whether or not or no longer or no longer they may be inclined to behave as guardians of your children, have to the need get up, earlier than you nominate them as such on your will.

Funeral preparations

List proper right here your funeral wishes.

Example:

I want to be cremated and my ashes to be sprinkled beneath the big very welltree next to the family home at (address).

Drafting your first will

I accept as proper with that after you have got have been given finished the muse above you're capable of draft your first will.

If you are going to kind your will on a pc, create a Word file and call it "Draft Will". If you'll write your will with the useful resource of manner of hand, select out A4 length paper. If you are writing your non-public will, a handwritten will is compulsory in global places like France. It is therefore critical to test your america's legal necessities for a valid will to ensure which you are allowed to type write your will.

Creating a typewritten will with Word makes it easy that allows you to paintings on, preserve, edit, amend, or rectify drafting errors for your draft will.

Now with the notes you have made above, collectively with the financial disaster on

"Essential Clauses" on this ebook, you're now armed and geared up to start drafting your very very own will.

Here is a chronological framework that you may use:

Commencement clause

Revocation clause

Clause appointing your executor

Distribution clauses

Start along facet your specific legacy clauses first and then address your residuary property final.

If you do no longer have legacy clauses, you can depart the complete of your private home to your selected beneficiaries.

Guardianship clause (if vital)

Burial desires

Attestation clause

Remember to additionally create a space at the lowest of every internet web page for you as testator further for your witnesses to sign.

If you are satisfied that this draft will encompass your testamentary desires you may keep to print it out.

Read it all all over again after you have posted it out. If you discover drafting errors, restoration the ones in the Word document, then preserve and print it all over again. Discard the primary located draft which had the mistakes. Save a backup reproduction of your Draft Will document on an outside memory deliver e.G., an out of doors difficult strength, reminiscence stick, or perhaps the cloud.

Execution

Once you are satisfied that the broadcast draft displays your testamentary goals correctly, you're geared up to have it completed. Literally all you need is a pen, ideally one with black ink, and in a function witnesses to witness your and every other's signatures at the same time as you're all in every exceptional's presence. With all 3 of you gift, inform the witnesses this is your last will and testomony and you need them to witness your and every one in every of a kind's signatures thru signing in the front of each specific. You as testator ought to sign first. Start with the useful resource of the usage of signing each web page of your will at the lowest thereof after which maintain up to now and sign the attestation clause as testator. Thereafter, offer the same pen to the primary witness and watch at the same time as she or he signs and symptoms and signs at the bottom of every internet internet page after which as first witness on the attestation clause. Thereafter, the second witness takes the pen and signs and symptoms as witness at the lowest of every internet page and then as second witness on the attestation clause.

Congratulations! You in reality wrote and carried out your first valid will!

If you need to make any changes on your closing will and testomony, the excellent advice I can offer you with is to simply clearly create a trendy one. Do now not write changes onto your performed will. If you do, the ones similarly writings can also moreover even must be validly completed. Just go to your Draft Will document in your computer, make the changes you need, shop it, print the document, proofread it, and then execute it once more within the presence of witnesses. This is also the same simple process to hold your will up to date. More approximately that inside the subsequent financial ruin. Once done, shop your will in a safe location and inform your executor or a depended on man or woman in which to discover it after your dying.

Chapter 5: Keeping your will up to date

Circumstances change over time. People get divorced, they get married, they have got children, their kids increase as much as be adults, they get grandchildren, family contributors pass away, and new ones get born. In quick, lifestyles takes area.

All the ones situations want to have an effect on your initial testamentary intentions. As a depend of fact, in some states and international locations, the act of having married or getting divorced mechanically revokes all previous wills you can have made. In different international places, it doesn't. One truth remains advantageous: whether or not your preceding will modified into robotically revoked with the useful resource of regulation or no longer, your occasions changed so appreciably that you are in dire want of a ultra-modern will.

I suggest which you evaluate your current will at the least as soon as every one year and on every occasion after a number one occasion to your lifestyles to ensure that the testamentary intentions contemplated therein are although your contemporary testamentary intentions. If now not, it's time to update your will.

You try this with the beneficial aid of growing a modern will, similar to we referred to in this manual, for you to revoke all preceding wills. In the times long past through, in advance than we had computer structures and phrase processors, this end up a tedious task, specially if you best wanted to make a minor exchange. As a cease stop result, testators used codicils to amend their wills. These days, there may be no want for codicils anymore. It is an awful lot much less complicated, less complicated, and masses much less confusing now to create a contemporary updated will and feature it executed.

Go for your Will file which you stored on your pc and with a bit of luck have moreover sponsored as tons as an external memory supply like a flash pressure or perhaps to the cloud. After carefully considering the amendments that need to be made, amend your initial draft will hence and maintain it beneath a one of a kind filename. I recommend the use of the date as part of the record name, for instance Draftwill20.Eleven.2021. Now print it out and proofread it. If there are not any drafting mistakes, continue to execute it in a right way inside the presence of witnesses as mentioned above inside the previous financial disaster. Once finished, save your will in a constant place together at the side of your previous wills.

Keep your vintage will. In the occasion of a dispute, and if the courtroom docket located that your present day-day will is invalid, your formerly legitimate felony will can be declared to be your last will and testomony. If there aren't any different wills, and the court docket pronounces your final will and testomony invalid, your property will bypass on intestacy.

It goes with out announcing that in case you had your will professionally drafted, you continue to need to hold your will up to date on a normal foundation. Most professional will drafters will price you a nominal fee if you installation with them to have your will reviewed on a every 12 months foundation and amended if desires be. As I said in advance than, cash spent on the services of a professional will drafter is coins properly invested to preserve your difficult-earned estate.

Chapter 6: Will Writing

Every time a person dies, the priority of will, if no longer immediately, short comes under talk. As poignant as the dearth of a loved one may be, the entirety a deceased leaves inside the back of needs to be treated. This ebook objectives to shed off a few burden of managing estate settlements and inheritance affairs within the hard time of loss. Before we plunge into the techniques and legalities of creating a will, we need to first recognize the fundamentals of will writing.

What is a Will?

A will or a testomony is a prison document that explains the wishes of someone, or a testator, to be greater accurate, approximately the distribution of the testator's wealth and property after his/her lack of lifestyles. It names one or more character as an executor to manipulate the property until disbursed in keeping with the desires of the testator.

A will gives people with a jail manner to distribute their property and wealth as they need to. However, this complete technique is every so often additionally ruled by using way of the laws of compelled heirship in many nations, in that you are legally restricted from disinheriting your partner or perhaps kids, in a few cases.

It is regularly wrongly assumed that a will is made to head away commands surely about the distribution of the testator's belongings. In fact, in your will, you may call a discern for your children and belongings, name an executor to govern your property and specific your desires approximately a manner to pay your money owed and taxes. A will also can useful resource a dwelling take delivery of as actual with.

Even although a will is a prison expression of your goals after your loss of life, a will does no longer have the authority of handling the distribution of non-probate property. Non-probate belongings, each thru the task of the law or because of an earlier agreement, will bypass right away to a person else subsequently after your death rather than turning into part of your property. We will have a examine it in addition in the financial disaster about beneficiaries.

The Legal Requirements of a Will

There are not many prison requirements for writing a will. You have all of the prison authority to put in writing your very very own will, and you may moreover lease a legal expert for it. You need to be privy to the belongings you have got, and you have to simply recognize what it manner to leave your home to someone else after your lifestyles. In criminal terms, it's far called having the functionality of creating a will because of this that being of sound mind. You want to also name beneficiaries for a number of your own home within the will. Moreover, you are legally required to signal the file of your will and get witnesses to signal it.

You are not legally sure to notarize your will, however getting a notarized self proving affidavit makes the stairs of probate much less complex. Notarizing a will consists of the testator and the witnesses to take an oath and sign a sworn declaration, maintaining that they have got signed the choice within the presence of the testator and vice-versa.

Although some global places acquire a handwritten will, they will be more liable to challenge after the testator's loss of life. Therefore, you want to opt for a handwritten will if you do not have the time to make a right one.

What Happens if a Person Dies Without a Will?

If someone dies without creating a will, the inheritance law of his/her u . S . Determines the distribution of assets and the human beings named thru the regulation get the inheritance through using default. These prison recommendations variety from u.S. To u . S . A ., however in maximum cases, the belongings is despatched the diverse partner and the kids. If the deceased does now not go away any associate or youngsters in the back of, then his property passes without delay to different own family contributors.

The manner in which the regulation distributes the belongings generally shows how most humans should want to distribute their assets after their demise. The problem for you might be which you could not need to distribute your private home inside the manner kingdom law does it. Making a will offers you the liberty of dishing out your private home consistent with your preference in preference to following a country determined default plan. In order to take manage of your lifetime assets and their distribution after your lifestyles, you must depart a will in order that your legacy lives on as in line with your choice.

The Right Time of Writing Your Will

Most humans hold casting off the venture of writing a will. Even even though it's far very well to put in writing your will at any age, there are a few incidences in lifestyles on the identical time as you have to prepare to install writing a will so you can make certain a secure and consistent destiny on your family and loved ones.

If you don't want your circle of relatives to address the tiresome mission of sorting your private home without your steerage after your existence, you need to especially make or reevaluate your will when you have sold new property. Purchasing a real property or any assets will increase the charge of your nation. This have to require you to declare for your will how your beneficiaries or your heirs might be affected by the increase within the fee of your estate. You may be required to assess how this new assets is probably allotted most of the heirs.

If you have already got a will at the same time as you get married, your marriage will revoke your will till you have got noted within the will that it'll stay powerful after your marriage. Furthermore, in case you get divorced, the talents of your will that consist of your ex-accomplice becomes null and void. It is vital after those sports activities of lifestyles to put in writing your will or revise it to wholesome the brand new conditions.

Another crucial event is the addition of a modern day member of the family in your existence. The starting of a little one requires you to revise or write your will to make certain which you encompass the current member of the family on your will and offer for his/her destiny.

If you revel in a near loss of life revel in, you ought to make a selection approximately the distribution of your house amongst your circle of relatives members and accomplice and kids. It is likewise advocated to revise your will each five years to address any primary existence sports, any changes in the law, further to adjustments in non-public priorities. If you have not made a will or revised it in masses of years, these activities have to encourage you to make that decision faster.

Chapter 7: Things to Consider in advance than Writing a Will

Once you have decided to make a will, you need to keep in mind many things which might be essential to put in writing a will. It is essential that you are familiar with the factors blanketed in a will and the way they have got an effect on your will. So, in advance than you put together a draft of your will, study the ones crucial factors of will writing.

Assets

Assets are all of the tangible and intangible such things as assets, financial savings and investments owned and managed through the use of you. Anything that has fee and is on your private possession is to be blanketed for your will. Assets which can be shared and are underneath joint possession cannot be covered in your will because of the reality they're vulnerable to the agreement that you have with the joint owner. In joint possession of an asset, property switch to the opposite owner in case of death of each owner. When you decide to write down a will, you need to first make a listing of all of your home and calculate their value. Calculating the fee is important because of the fact there might be a few financial and tax obligations to be completed for the method of creating a will.

Along together together with your property, you could moreover provide an reason for to your will what your desires regarding the disposal of your body are. You can deliver precise commands approximately your funeral and also can donate your organs to shop one of a kind lives.

Beneficiaries

A beneficiary is essentially any man or woman or entity who gets the cash or assets due to the fact you have got named them for your will. There's a distinction among heirs and beneficiaries. An inheritor is your blood relative this is entitled by using manner of default to get coins or belongings you very personal after your dying. A beneficiary additionally can be a chum or can encompass donations and charities, a place of worship or perhaps a doggy.

When it entails beneficiaries, the question that arises is who need to advantage from your house. The obvious solution usually includes accomplice and youngsters. However, there are extra topics to consider in this trouble. You also can deal with special situations for your will, which include decreasing out estranged children, if your accomplice can remarry and disinherit your children, what takes region if every your partner and youngsters bypass away and if you may consist of your children from the alternative marriage. You can deal with all of the situations you need to embody concerning your beneficiaries of the want.

Executors

An executor can be every body you name in you could to carry out the responsibilities of property distribution for your house after your loss of lifestyles. Spouse or children are frequently desired by using the usage of most humans to be decided on as executors. But, when you have a doubt that your children may also get proper proper into a conflict later, you may select someone out of your own family or a expert executor for the project. You also can choose out an alternative to your executor so that in his absence or in case of his demise, the artificial can execute the distribution.

If your youngsters are minor, you can pick out out a trustee for them to control your estate until your kids are of age to inherit it. Executors can also play the characteristic of a trustee. Moreover, if your children are minor, you could furthermore need to call guardians to attend to your children. It is not important that their parent, trustee or executor of your will is the identical man or woman. You can select awesome people however ensure that they pass properly together with every unique because of the fact they may must coordinate often. You want to undergo in mind that despite the fact that you could name multiple executor, it desires more paper paintings and there is constantly a hazard of warfare between the two executors. A bank can also play the placement of an executor but you can need to pay a difficult and fast rate for its offerings.

An executor does now not have the authority to promote your real property with out getting court docket's approval. However, if you remember your executor and do no longer doubt his intentions; you can supply your executor the authority of promoting your real assets without courtroom's permission.

Witnesses

In most states, there are to be two witnesses to your will. In a few states, the variety of witnesses might also moreover variety in a number of the international locations in the global. But in US, UK, Canada, Australia and South Africa, the kind of witnesses is . Ensure that each the witnesses are adults and are of sound thoughts. These witnesses should not be beneficiaries in your will. Some states allow beneficiaries to be witnesses but it's far better to have separate witnesses to keep away from the problem of undue have an impact on.

Self Approved Affidavit

A self authorized affidavit is a separate sheet of paper linked with the desire. It is signed and notarized at the time at the equal time as the want is signed and witnessed. A self established affidavit legally validates your will. If your will has notarized self authorised affidavit with it, it's far probated proper away without having the need to touch the witnesses.

On the possibility hand, in case your will does no longer have a self authorised affidavit together with it, the courtroom docket does no longer admit it to probate until it's miles proved that the need is actual. This may be an prolonged approach because of the fact the witnesses can be contacted to affirm the validity of the choice. If the witnesses aren't available, a person else will ought to confirm that it's far a actual will made via you.

However, it isn't obligatory to notarize your will. If you do now not have enough time or it is not feasible on the way to attain a notary, you may as properly make the preference without a notary. A notarized self permitted affidavit simplest makes the method an entire lot plenty less complicated and quicker to show the validity of your will inside the court.

Making a will is a hard company. In order to probate the selection, it's far essential that it's far easy of all suspicion and doubts. Ensure that there are not any rub out or erased additives for your will. If you do have a few correction marked on the need, you and the witnesses want to preliminary or signal it. Your will should have web page numbers stated at the lowest of each page and the notarized self permitted affidavit need to moreover be covered in those numbered pages a good manner to encompass it as a part of your will. All the pages of your will need to be signed or initialed through you further to the witnesses.

Disinheritance

By writing your will, you can determine who can gain out of your own home. Similarly, your will also can decide if there are any folks who will now not accumulate any provisions out of your home. If to your will, you specially exclude someone who might get preserve of from your home in any other case, this is referred to as disinheritance.

There are techniques of disinheriting a person; intentionally or by way of twist of fate. An intentional disinheritance is a announcement in your will which you go away not anything for that particular individual; like disinheriting an estranged son or daughter.

Accidental disinheritance takes area due to conditions that you didn't count on. For instance, you call an asset to your daughter and your financial institution account on your son. But, after your loss of lifestyles the asset receives provided because of any reason and the selling price of the asset is going into your monetary institution account leaving your daughter disinherited.

Usually, a partner cannot be disinherited absolutely. However, any of your kids can be disinherited through really bringing up to your will to exclude your son or daughter from the provisions of your property.

Chapter 8: Things that can Affect Your Will

You need to realize earlier than writing your will that your will isn't always a final word that can't be modified. There are a few procedures that make your will null and void or revoke it. The maximum fundamental manner to revoke your will is to ruin your will or make a contemporary day will, really bringing up in it which you revoke the previous one. There are a few different things which can have an impact to your will so you may be referred to in element in this bankruptcy.

Marriage

While you may deliberately revoke your personal will, marriage revokes your will automatically until you have got have been given mentioned in the will that it remains unaffected through marriage. The regulation in most global places therefore wishes that you upload in a assertion that the want is to live powerful to the beneficiaries after your marriage. Doing this protects your will from being revoked. If you would love to marry a selected individual, you could upload a assertion in your will that your will shall live legitimate after your marriage with that man or woman. It is higher to say the choice of the character you're to marry.

Divorce

Divorce impacts your will otherwise in particular states. In some legal pointers, divorce routinely revokes your will on the equal time as in others it first-rate invalidates the feature of your ex-accomplice as an executor or revokes his/her claim to any of the gives you named them for your will. If you're separated but no longer legally divorced, all of the provisions of your will to your estranged partner will continue to be legitimate. If you die even as separated but now not divorced, your estranged accomplice gets all of the provisions mentioned in the will.

After you're legally divorced, the conditions regarding your ex-companion turns into invalid. If you had formerly named your ex-partner as an executor in advance than the divorce, that clause may also grow to be void and the change executor will have to tackle the position. The last will would probable remain unaffected and truely legitimate. The a part of your property which you had named on your ex-associate will pass immediately to the alternate beneficiaries cited inside the will.

A divorce will now not revoke your will surely however it is an essential occasion in existence. Your dreams regarding the distribution of your property would possibly likely considerably alternate, consequently, it's miles recommended to revise your will after your divorce. If you skip away even as you have were given been divorced and you had no longer revised the desire, your ex-partner can also moreover inherit the property you named to them to your will. Likewise, in case you had named your ex-accomplice as an executor however did not change it after your divorce, your ex-accomplice is probably able to play that function relying at the regulation of your u . S ..

Will Disputes

Will disputes have turn out to be more common than they ever had been inside the beyond and that they have got a extensive impact on the need. There are kinds of will disputes within the wider scope of factors. You can both venture or contest a will.

Challenging is claiming within the courtroom that the need itself is invalid because of any shape of motives just like the man or woman no longer being sound at the time of writing their will. The different type of will dispute is contesting the want because of this that that the want does now not make a logical financial provision.

Your will may be challenged to be invalid through a person at the grounds of:

Lack of knowledge: It may be claimed that while the individual had the complete capability of creating a will, they did no longer completely recognize or approve of what the selection certainly contained.

Undue effect: It can be claimed that you have been underneath undue have an effect on on the time of creating your will. This way that you had been manipulated via the use of a third birthday celebration even as developing a will.

Fraud: After you pass away, it could be claimed that your signature on the selection grow to be cast. This approach that your will modified into changed by using using way of a person and the signature come to be stable to make it seem like your will.

In maximum global locations, the inheritance regulation has a provision for circle of relatives and dependants. This permits someone to contest your will within the occasion that they feel that an low-fee provision emerge as now not made for them to your will whilst they had been your own family or dependant.

These claims commonly have to be made brief after the need comes into effect (i.E. After your death). Usually, there is a limited time to make these claims that is generally round 6 months. After that, you want to take permission of the court docket docket docket to make this type of declare.

Revocation of a Will

As said in advance, making a brand new will revokes your antique will with the situation that you include a statement for your new will that you revoke all former wills formerly made via you. If you pass over out this announcement to your new will, there will nonetheless be an implied revocation of all former wills if you have covered all your own home or belongings for your new will.

Another way to revoke your very own will is to damage the preference your self with the aim of revoking it. You can also ask someone to damage it however it is vital that it is done to your presence and you honestly country to that character that you intend to break the preference to revoke it.

There is a danger which you with the resource of threat spoil your will through destroying your or the witnesses' signature but if the aim modified into no longer to revoke it, it'll however live legitimate. Accidentally or accidentally destroying the need does not revoke the want in step with regulation. If you misplace or mislay your will, it will still be powerful regardless. Only creating a trendy will and mentioning in it that you revoke all former wills previously made through you may revoke your out of area will.

Thus, it's miles crucial to undergo in thoughts all of the elements that may have any shape of impact on your will earlier than developing a will.

Chapter 9: Beneficiaries of your Will

One of the maximum essential additives of writing a will is to decide who will advantage from your estate and property. As stated, earlier beneficiaries are the human beings and entities that get preserve of a proportion in your private home through your will. This chapter discusses the only-of-a-kind classes of the beneficiaries in detail and the topics related to them.

Beneficiaries can be divided into following large classes:

Primary Beneficiaries

A primary beneficiary is the most simple form of beneficiary who advantages out of your will. These are the human beings or entities that you right now call to your will for certain portions of your private home. Primary beneficiaries may be any or all the following kinds:

Spouse

The first actual interest even as doling out your house is generally the immediate own family of the character growing a will. Even greater so, a partner is often the number one beneficiary named in a will. The regulation in masses of states also prevents you from disinheriting your spouse on your will. You can also additionally name everything for your accomplice but take into account the capability of your spouse to manipulate your home and providing in your dependents after your dying.

Children

While you have got were given the liberty of leaving the entirety to your partner's arms to offer in your youngsters as well, you could moreover consist of positive provisions to your kids on your will. It is important to deal with a situation wherein some component takes location in your partner. Moreover, if you or your associate have children from another marriage, you want to genuinely make unique provisions to your kids on your will.

Relatives and Friends

Relatives also may be a part of your will if you desire. Often, people want to offer for his or her siblings or mother and father, nieces or nephews, and so forth. You can create specific provisions in your circle of relatives from your property for your will. Apart from circle of relatives and loved ones, some near pals additionally may be beneficiaries in your will. You can provide for them for your will as you desire.

Charities

Charities additionally may be beneficiaries for your will. Charities rely upon donations and often those donations come as affords from estates. You can designate some part of your property to charitable organizations and entities that paintings for social provider and betterment of the society. This way you may assist advantage the network even after your dying. The tax laws in remarkable international locations moreover encourage gadgets out of your house for charities. This permits to lessen profits and property tax on the value of your estate.

Alternate Beneficiaries

Alternate or contingent beneficiaries are some special elegance of beneficiaries. They are individuals named on your will which is probably to gain out of your house if the primary beneficiary cannot gather the provision due to any purpose or refuse to take it. You want to consist of on your will that who might be your preference in case your primary beneficiary does no longer continue to exist. So, in case your number one beneficiary cannot get keep of your provisions, you need to name a contingent beneficiary who can get that provision in any other case. Your will must consist of sufficient exchange beneficiaries to make sure that beneficiaries is probably to be had to collect the supply of your property.

Beneficiaries of Joint Legacies

Another category of beneficiaries are the beneficiaries of joint legacies or shared presents. A joint legacy or shared gift is any present or provision that you offer through your will to be shared amongst or greater human beings. The beneficiaries receiving this shared present come to be joint tenants of that gift. Rather than proudly proudly owning a share in the present, joint tenants private the present virtually. The joint tenants have the selection to every at the same time observe divide the present or maintain proudly proudly owning it together. This way that each one the joint tenants will want to agree in advance than taking any choice approximately the triumphing. One individual can not take the selection of selling the triumphing on his non-public.

A shared present can also take shipping of to tenants in commonplace via your will. Tenants in common way that each one the tenants of the present will nice have a share inside the gift and no one will absolutely personal it. You can call a gift to be shared unequally amongst tenants in not unusual. The joint tenants are at liberty to unanimously conform to alternate to being tenants in commonplace. This will change the whole ownership of the present to same percent of the gift between the tenants.

Residuary Beneficiaries

You can designate your specific assets to primary beneficiary. Then, in desire to list the whole belongings, you may thing out in your will that every other beneficiary will obtain the relaxation of your estate. This beneficiary receiving the last property is known as the residuary beneficiary. You also can call trade residuary beneficiary to call a person who gets keep of this last part of property if the residuary beneficiary passes away. This guarantees that there are sufficient beneficiaries for the deliver of your home.

Naming beneficiaries for the availability of your house to your will is an critical component of creating a will. You need to provide an lousy lot attention to all the beneficiaries you're to encompass on your will and offer change beneficiaries for them as it ought to be. Major changes in life like a wedding, divorce, start of a little one or lack of lifestyles of a beneficiary of your will call for changes to be made in your will.

Chapter 10: Write Your Own Will

Whether you are married, a discern or someone with out kids, there are some vital hints of will writing that remain identical. To be amazing that your will is valid, you want to be over 18 years of age and also you need to sign your will within the front of witnesses. The witnesses must also sign the desire on the identical time. Another primary requirement for writing your will is which you have to be of sound thoughts and understand your will actually. If you have got employed a attorney to get criminal help in writing your will, your legal professional need to make sure that you are mentally in a role. It is likewise essential that you simply u . S . A . To your will what you reason to do with all of your private home. More often than not, problems in a probate approach stand up because of ambiguity and obscurity in the will. This economic catastrophe will talk some preferred and a few precise commands approximately writing your non-public will.

Estate Planning for a Married Person

One of the maximum important things to don't forget as soon as you have got married is belongings making plans. This is to make certain that your associate and kids are provided for correctly in case some thing takes location to you. An property plan consists of a hard and fast of files that specify after dying desires and whole commands approximately the manner to distribute your house.

A marriage alters your monetary and crook fame in exclusive ways. As a lifestyles partner, you may share your earnings, assets, bank account and plenty of others. You are also able to record joint taxes with your associate. You can be recognized as a married couple legally.

After marriage, you may have distinct sorts of houses: separate and marital assets. Separate assets is the assets truely owned with the aid of you and your accomplice has no possession of it while marital assets is the property which you percent at the aspect of your partner and it is at the identical time owned among you and your associate. So, if there are assets or some belongings which you need to very very personal independently, you could make a prenuptial settlement or region this assets one by one in a consider.

There are strategies the belongings of a married couple is despatched amongst spouses after lack of lifestyles or divorce in high-quality global places. The assets is each handled as community assets or equitable distribution is resorted to. Community property or network of property (as it's far diagnosed in South Africa) is a marital property regime which states that when a associate dies, the residing associate gets the percentage of the assets of the deceased accomplice whilst the separate assets of the deceased associate is sent in keeping with his/her will. In community assets states, the money owed are also shared most of the spouses.

On the opposite hand, equitable distribution is the marital property regime in which after loss of life or divorce, the regulation considers a difficult and speedy of things to distribute the marital property pretty maximum of the spouses. This cut up of belongings may be greater or much less than 1/2 of, depending on the jurisdiction. The elements that the court docket docket considers consist of profits and monetary contribution of both the spouses, the time that the couple has been married, the financial situation of the surviving accomplice and the economic needs of the dependants, and lots of others. In this regime, the debts are categorized like separate and shared belongings.

Writing a Will

Once you absolutely recognize all the factors of your house in marriage and the law approximately marital assets in your state, you could start developing your very own property plans. You need to include your partner on this manner. If your circle of relatives shape is simple and you or your spouse does now not have any youngsters aside from from your marriage, the two of you could create reciprocal or replicate wills. Mirror wills are separate wills for absolutely everyone however they replicate each different. It is also endorsed that you speak what you anticipate to take area to your home and belongings after loss of life at the side of how your private home need to be allocated at the side of your companion.

Following are some of the crucial elements of writing a will while you're married.

Deciding Guardianship for your Minor Children

The first essential detail to include in your will pertains to the guardianship of your minor kids. If you bypass away, your children can be sorted through the usage of way of the surviving associate. With that said, however, you and your companion ought to make a joint choice of naming a parent if every of you skip away. You can name a guardian and a co-dad or mum in your will for your minor children. You also can call multiple guardian in case one is not in a role to take care of your youngsters. Discuss and remember the possibility of a guardian along side your spouse. Ensure that your preferred mother or father is capable of looking after your children's intellectual, bodily, and economic nicely-being. Inform your preferred mother or father about your preference, speak his/her responsibilities, and make sure that the named mother or father has the identical opinion to all sincerely.

If your kids are adults then you definitely don't want to name any father or mother for them for your will.

Distribution of Marital and Separate Property

Bank debts, property, organization belongings and awesome belongings that is collectively shared by means of way of you and your spouse come under the class of marital assets. If certainly certainly one of you passes away, the deceased companion's percentage may be transferred to the surviving spouse in step with the regulation to your u.S.A. Of america. The guidelines of the country may even decide whether or no longer your property can be treated as community or equitable belongings. This switch of the deceased associate percent of marital belongings cannot be constant with the terms of his/her will; as an alternative it's going to rely upon the regulation of the usa. You can speak collectively together with your partner that what takes area on your marital property if every of you pass away simultaneously.

Although every the humans in a couple are entitled to simplest their percent of marital assets, every of you may determine to provide an asset at the identical time shared via you to gift it to a person. Both of you could want to embody the same need on your wills. For marital belongings, it's miles critical that you and your partner paintings together and take the equal choice. It eases the technique of distribution of your property after your dying. If you very very very own assets collectively together with your spouse as tenants in commonplace, it manner that you best have a specific percent of the belongings so that you can encompass in your will to offer your percentage of that belongings to any beneficiary you pick out out.

For separate property and belongings, you can present them to whoever you want. You will have to country the belongings and the beneficiary to your will.

Wishes Regarding Health Care

Another critical element to encompass to your will is your want about your fitness care. It is critical to provide a fitness care directive to your will so in case you turn out to be disabled or unwell to allow others realize approximately your consent concerning particular remedies, your will may be a manual for them to offer you with the remedy steady in conjunction with your goals. In marriage, your associate has the prison authority to make selections for you. However, you can additionally hire someone else with Medical Power of Attorney. After consisting of those desires about your healthcare to your will, talk your picks along with your accomplice and your fitness care consultant so that everybody concerned is aware your options. You can encompass as lots element as you want however some not unusual factors are your preferred excellent of existence, your consent about synthetic lifestyles help, and your preference approximately surgical tactics, organ donation, and so forth.

Estate Planning for a Parent

A figure's duty to look after their children is not constrained to their lifetime most effective. In truth, as a determine, you need to make certain to provide on your youngsters even after you bypass away. This will not be lots one-of-a-kind than a normal will. The only addition could be your kids as beneficiaries on your will and imparting a guardian if they will be minor. The following elements might be vital in case you are a determine and you are writing your very personal will.

Deciding Guardianship for your Minor Children

As noted in the phase for assets making plans for a married character, you may determine a mother or father to your kids if they will be minors. It is a difficult choice because of the fact it is tough to anticipate a person else searching after your youngsters. Discuss your choice together with your associate and the chosen dad or mum. Ensure that the chosen parent is flawlessly able to taking the duties and has the equal opinion to them. You also can call an trade determine if considered one in every of them isn't always capable of anticipate the duty because of any purpose after your demise.

Distribution of your Property

In the following step, you will be thinking about all your own home that do not automatically switch to a beneficiary. All such monetary institution bills, property, houses, and so on may be named on your children to your will. You may additionally need to specify the age at which they could be able to have get admission to to their inheritance if they're more youthful. In the meantime, you could assign a father or mother or each different person to control your property. You can also entrust a financial institution to control your property until your kids are adults.

Choose an Executor

You also can name an executor to your will to deal with the subjects regarding your house after you've got exceeded away. A dad or mum of your youngsters additionally may be assigned as an executor however ensure who ever you select out is able to taking the sort of responsibility and consents to take it. If you have not named any executors for your will, the courtroom would probable assign one to expect the duties of an executor.

Estate Planning for a Person without a Children

It is critical to do assets making plans and writing a may moreover even when you have no youngsters or heirs to distribute it amongst. If you die without a will and you have no kids, your house and belongings are dispensed consistent with the law of your country. These suggestions may not be in step with your wishes so it is crucial to draft a will so that your tough earned cash goes to someone you need to collect. In maximum country prison hints of inheritance, there's usually a ladder of who receives your home when you die without a will and children. If you don't have any children and you possibly did not write a will earlier than passing away, your private home will move on for your companion. If you go away no associate, it gets allotted amongst your parents and in case you haven't any dad and mom each, your siblings inherit your private home automatically. So, if you need to save you this hard scenario, you need to write a will for the distribution of your home steady together along with your needs.

Choose an Executor

Like otherwise of writing a will, you may ought to select an executor to perform the needs for your will. This can embody retitling or charge of taxes. In case you haven't any youngsters, you may choose out out a near pal or a relative as an executor of your will. Ensure that they're willing and capable to carry out the ones obligations.

Choose a Charity as a Beneficiary

Having no kids doesn't exchange masses of the additives of writing a will. You can however entitle your spouse, parents, siblings, buddies or cherished ones to get your own home after your loss of life as you preference. However, when you have quite a few property and belongings to get rid of, you may furthermore pick out a charity or a donation to bypass on your private home to. It does no longer handiest satisfy your social responsibility but can also benefit you financially in actual life. Donating your own home to a charity lowers your own home tax payments. You can write down the commands approximately how your house may be transferred to the charity and additionally set apart some amount for your will for the executor to get tax consultation concerning your private home this is to be donated after your lifestyles.

Health Care and Financial Decisions

Another component to be included in a will for a childless individual is who will take health and financial options for him if he will become incapacitated to make the ones picks. Ideally, you could call your associate to make those selections for you if the want arises. But if you have no accomplice or anyways you may call an alternate as nicely who should make health care and economic picks for you. It may be your sibling, relative, pal or everybody who you could trust.

Conclusively, those are 3 precise instances of writing a will. The sizable hints of writing a will live the equal in all instances. In any case, it's far vital to speak about the essential topics of your will collectively with your companion and children for the cause that doing so will make the distribution of your home after your loss of existence simpler. After writing, signing and testifying the desire, hold it in a strong region. You can tell your partner, executors and health care representative approximately wherein your will is saved.

Chapter 11: What to Include to your Will

Writing your own will within reason easy and easy. You can purchase a will shape from a stationery store or maybe download a will template from the internet to get commenced. You may additionally want to get greater sheets because the distance for the provisions of a will won't suffice.

Sometimes, a new will is written and you clearly overlook approximately your vintage will. There is one clause which you need to consist of each time you write a present day-day will; i.E. "I revoke all former wills and codicils and testamentary provisions." This is essential because in case you make a contemporary will and you have were given had been given neither destroyed the antique one nor introduced this revocation clause in the new will, it locations a question mark on the validity of the present day will. Both the want are then proved and the combined provisions of every the wills are implemented. The following are the primary topics to include for your will, within the identical order.

Opening Statements

You must start out via writing the hole statement of your will; i.E. "This is the ultimate will and testament of (full name)." This assertion want to consist of your complete name, modern-day cope with and the date on which you are writing the need. The next statement to characteristic is that you revoke all preceding wills, codicils and testamentary provisions.

Naming an Executor and Guardian

The next trouble is to call a non-public representative or an executor who is probably responsible to perform your final desires as in keeping with your will. An executor may be someone or an organisation. You can also call change executors as properly here in case one fails to perform those responsibilities due to any motive. You may also encompass in this clause if the executor is to be paid and the way he/she need to be paid.

Moreover, in case your children are minor and you have not declared a person as their mum or dad after your loss of existence, then you definately must consist of that during your will as properly. It can encompass the greater instructions you need to encompass for the figure about your children's care.

Wishes about Funeral Arrangements

After naming the executor and parent, you can united states of america any particular dreams (if any) about your funeral arrangements. However, funeral dreams said inside the will are not legally binding.

A own family may additionally have already made the funeral preparations in advance than they come upon your will.

Testamentary Expenses

Testamentary fees are all of the fees which can be incurred on the administration of the property until it's miles allocated some of the beneficiaries. It additionally includes repayment for the executors or personal representatives. You want to united states of america that all the property or testamentary charges need to be paid via way of the assets. At this component, you need to additionally element out that if the gifts furnished via the choice are freed from inheritance tax liabilities. If you need these objects to be free of inheritance tax, then you definately in fact have to provide an amount for the tax while calculating the valuation of your private home.

Naming Beneficiaries for Specific Bequests

In this subsequent step, you may name particular gadgets of belongings, like coins, assets, actual property to all of us you want. Mostly, human beings name their partner, youngsters and distinct partner and children for the ones particular bequests. But, you could additionally call it to buddies, business business enterprise partners, charities, agencies, and plenty of others. You need to nation it like; "I deliver and bequeath the following legacy to (names) of (deal with)." You ought to specifically u.S. About the present that a beneficiary is to obtain and if it's far a real belongings or land, you need to moreover specify its region. You want to maintain on collectively with different bequests in the same way.

Mentioning Alternate Beneficiaries

You can then go on to name alternate beneficiaries on your bequests. Your will should u.S. Of america what should rise up to your own home if a particular beneficiary does no longer stay on. You can name an trade beneficiary similar to the man or woman's partner or kids or a person not related to the genuine beneficiary.

Naming Residuary Beneficiary

After naming beneficiaries for precise bequests, you want to do away with those belongings or assets that you have not given to all and sundry; i.E. The residuary belongings. The residuary belongings will visit this beneficiary after the inheritance tax has been paid and all distinct testamentary expenses had been deducted. The suitable announcement to characteristic for this is "I devise and bequeath the residue of my real and non-public belongings to (name) of (cope with).' You can add a survivorship clause with this this is if this beneficiary does no longer live on 30 days (or any style of days as you need); it need to bypass directly to some other named person.

Payment of Debts, Expenses, and Taxes

You need to additionally deliver an explanation for the way you want your debts, testamentary fees and inheritance taxes to be settled. You need to additionally point out about the monetary organization account a terrific way to cover some of these payments.

Instructions about Maintaining Real Estate

You also can encompass any particular commands approximately how to maintain your actual property. This clause is truly optionally to be had and you may depart it out when you have no precise instructions approximately its upkeep.

Attestation Clause

The closing hassle to embody for your will is the attestation clause. In this clause, you can united states of america, "Signed with the aid of the stated testator inside the presence folks gift on the same time and thru using us in his/her presence.' You and the two witnesses will signal right here. It is also vital that the witnesses write their entire names in addition to addresses with the signature.

Every will has wonderful content due to the fact the instances and goals of all and sundry variety. So a married person with kids may have wonderful needs and opportunities than someone without children. Therefore, aside from the favored factors of the need, the content material also can range from person to person.

Chapter 12: Finalizing your Will

Once you have were given included all the clauses cited inside the final chapter, you are almost accomplished along with your will writing mission. However, this remaining step might be one of the most vital steps. It should be finished with great care and hobby due to the fact it may make your will invalid otherwise. You must signal your will in the presence of your witnesses and notary public in case you are planning to self-approve it to. On the other hand, the witnesses should additionally sign your will at the same time in the presence of each you and the notary public's.

Review your Will

You must evaluation your will one extra time in advance than signing it. This will make certain that you haven't overlooked any vital element or no longer a few thing is contrary for your needs. You can print out a draft of your will if you have typed it and then evaluate it very well earlier than signing.

Signing of the Will

It is important that every one the parties; i.E. The testator and the 2 witnesses signal the preference in every special's presence. Both the witnesses need to be present whilst every body signs and symptoms the want. The law requires the witnesses to be of 18 years or older and that they need to moreover be of sound thoughts. It is appropriate to now not use a beneficiary as witnesses even though he/she is an change beneficiary. This is to keep away from battle of interest. Since, whilst you skip away the witnesses will testify your will inside the direction of probate, so it's miles higher to pick out out witnesses who are in particular health and are ideally more youthful than you. Moreover, factor out the deal with of the witnesses with their names so it's far a good deal less difficult to the touch them at some point of probate.

Self-Proving Affidavit

As cited previously within the e book, that attaching a self-proving affidavit with the desire is an crucial task in finalizing your will. This technique which you and the witnesses will sign the preference inside the presence of a notary public. Your will might be despite the fact that valid although it is not feasible to try this inside the presence of a notary public however it delays the probate machine. Once the testator and the witnesses have signed the choice, they're to sign the self-proving affidavit as well and the notary will notarize it. Without a self-proving affidavit, the court calls for the witnesses to seem within the front of the court or deliver a sworn assertion that the selection is legitimate and real. On the alternative hand, if the choice has the affidavit related to it, the validity of the preference does no longer ought to be proved to the courtroom docket. This makes the probate way a whole lot quicker.

Professional Consultation

You also can as properly want an criminal professional or a tax expert to study your will. This will make certain that there aren't any troubles with the crook implications of your choices. People with severa belongings or have a few unusual options approximately the distribution in their belongings, are advocated to get a professional consultation. It is properly surely well worth noting although which you have your very non-public first-class advice to your options about your will. So, until you enjoy it essential, you can flow on to install writing your will and get it attested in your private.

Altering the Will

After you and the witnesses have signed the need, it is vital which you do not regulate the desire in any manner. Do no longer insert any written or typed modifications for your will and do not even accurate the misspelled phrases. Any changes within the will need to be made by using using following the identical approach of signing and witnessing as that of the specific will. As stated earlier that it's far allowed to make corrections earlier than signing the desire, however it have to be averted besides important. Corrections create doubts for the probate court docket docket that whether or not or no longer the corrections were made earlier than or after signing the choice. If you made the corrections after signing the need, it's going to make your will invalid. For modifications, you may both make a brand new will or make a right trade thru attaching a codicil for your will.

Storing your Will

The final step of finalizing your will is to hold it in a secure area, ideally in a fireproof discipline. It ought to be with out issue reachable for your heirs and your executor want to be aware in which you have have been given stored it safe. If you're close to your youngsters and acquire as real with them, you can additionally ask one in all them to preserve it in a solid deposit subject.

These steps will assist you in finalizing your will and making it legitimate. The self-proving affidavit will essentially make the probate way quicker and less hard for your heirs and executor alike.

Chapter 13: All You Need to Know About Wills

A will is an tool acquainted thru law that lets in any person of sound mind to dispose, provide and bequeath all or a restrained portion of his homes, rights and duties to 1 or extra man or woman, natural or juridical, after his death.

The character who writes the need is referred to as the testator. The character or folks who receives maintain of his houses are referred to as the heirs or legatees. The one with a purpose to execute the provision of the need is referred to as the executor.

What can be disposed, given and bequeathed in a will?

Unless the regulation especially offer otherwise, all of the houses, rights and duties of the character may be disposed, given and bequeathed via him to any individual he selected to be his heir or legatees.

Future homes, rights and obligations, which the testator can also moreover get maintain of or recognize after writing the want and after his death, also can be disposed, given and bequeathed thru him.

Who can write or create a Will?

Anyone who is of sound thoughts can write or create a will. However, a few global places or states offer a selected age limit in advance than someone can write a will.

Some international locations allow a joint will. A Joint will is one this is written or created through or more folks.

Who can be an heir or legatee?

Any man or woman, herbal or juridical, in sound or unsound thoughts, can be an heir or a legatee to a will except:

1.   Any character who tried to kill the testator and determined responsible of fraud inside the route of the latter after the execution of the need;

If the enterprise of the heir have become made thru the testator prior to the commission of the crime towards him, the organization of the inheritor may be deemed invalid. If the institution of the inheritor turned into made after the rate of the crime, the corporation can be deemed legitimate and may be deemed as a pardon given via the testator.

2.   The mistress or paramour of the testator, specifically if the prison companion is unnoticed from the choice;

Mistresses or paramours of the testators might not be instituted as heirs as they may be in opposition to the morals. However, there have been instances even as judicial courts allowed mistresses and paramours to be named as heirs especially when the crook associate expressly abandoned the testator and it modified into the mistress or the paramour who supported the testator.

3. Persons who are however to be conceived;

Future grandchildren cannot be named as heirs thru a grandfather. The child need to be conceived first before they'll be instituted as heirs.

Minors, mentally incapacitated, and mentally-unwell human beings can be named as heirs and can get hold of their inheritances thru the parent or man or woman super via the testator. If one have end up not particular, the probate court or the executor may additionally additionally designate a felony determine.

In a few countries, unborn youngsters additionally can be made an heir or legatee furnished that:

1. The determine or parents of the unborn kids is sure within the will;

2. The unborn infant is born alive; if the child is born in advance, the child should live for twenty-four hours earlier than being taken into consideration to have been born alive;

three. The unborn children had been conceived at the time of the writing of the preference and/or at some stage in the lifestyles of the testator.

For juridical human beings, like charitable or academic foundations, the inheritance or legacies may be ordinary through the use of their duly prison person.

People with civil interdictions, inclusive of folks that are sentenced to imprisonment, can although be instituted as heirs. However, their company can be suspended until they regain their civil rights.

When does a will take impact?

A will takes impact upon the loss of lifestyles of the testator. However, if the law calls for that the want have to be probated, then the testamentary provisions therein may best be effected after the probate intending

If the regulation does not require any probate, the testamentary provisions inside the will are right now effective and executory upon the death of the testator.

Why is a Will crucial?

In many nations, a will does no longer get used the least bit. This is because of the reality the selection is inclined. A unmarried invalid or illegal provision might also moreover claim the will useless or invalid.

Still, there are numerous motives why writing a will is vital. Some of these reasons are stated below.

1. It can robust the testator's minor youngsters. This is the top reason why people execute wills.

Minors are regularly disregarded in the distribution of legitimes or their jail inheritance. With the desire, the testator can successfully switch the legitimes of his youngsters in a take delivery of as genuine with fund in order that no individual can be able to contact it or squander it from them.

2. It avoids struggle among heirs. Without a will, the houses, rights and obligations of the decedent are transferred robotically and further to his compulsory heirs. Since they have got same rights, conflicts can

also upward push up as to who will administer or can have manage over the homes.

3. It is a remarkable manner of paying gratitude to amazing humans. If there can be no will, the houses are routinely given to the obligatory heirs. The decedent may not have the opportunity to pay gratitude to his friends or his extraordinary circle of relatives humans. With the selection, he can appropriate a part of his homes to the opposite humans he loves.

four. It is a prison file to installation and apprehend a proper of someone. A will is may be used to installation and recognize an illegitimate infant. It additionally may be used to installation a proper to a creditor to gather from the property of the testator.

Kinds of Written Wills

There are   kinds of written will which is probably appreciably famous beneath International regulation. These are the holographic will and the notarial will.

The Holographic Will

The holographic will is one this is handwritten and signed for my part with the aid of the testator. It does not need to comply with any technicalities or form. The testator can write his will in any manner he prefers and in any piece of paper, supplied that every paper is signed and dated.

The greater essential aspect in writing a holographic will is its testamentary provisions.

The Notarial Will

The notarial will is one that is made through using the testator with the aid of a prison solicitor or a notary public. This type of will follows a particular shape or technique prescribed with the aid of the regulation of the land wherein the desire is being completed or the country wide regulation of the testator.

This form of will wishes to be signed thru the testator, attested via witnesses and stated earlier than a notary public, a prison solicitor or consul.

Any holographic will which the testator delivered about to be attested with the aid of the use of witnesses and recounted earlier than a notary public, a legal solicitor or consul is automatically deemed to have been transformed to a notarial will. However, the holographic portion of the choice can despite the fact that be widespread regardless of the truth that it does no longer conform to the prescribed form or system.

Chapter 14: Testamentary Provisions

Testamentary provisions are the statements furnished via the testator in his will. The future testator want to understand about testamentary provisions so that you can write an powerful final will and testament.

There are varieties of provisions that a testator may additionally include in his will. These are unconditional or absolute provisions and conditional provisions.

Unconditional or Absolute Provisions

If testamentary provision is unconditional or absolute, the inheritor or heirs do not have to do any act to qualify as an heir.

An instance of this testamentary provision is a smooth declaration which says,"I deliver and bequeath my house to Miley in Alabama." Upon the lack of lifestyles of the testator, Miley gets the house in Alabama.

Conditional Testamentary Provisions

If the testamentary provision is conditional, the inheritor or heirs may also need to do or forestall to do some aspect in advance than they're capable of qualify as an inheritor or legatee.

There are forms of conditional testamentary provisions that a testator can also additionally embody in his will. They are thesuspensive state of affairs, and resolutory conditions.

The Suspensive Conditional Testamentary Provisions

In the suspensive conditional testamentary provision, the instituted inheritor need to do, now not do or supply a few component in a big period in advance than he can get the inheritance.

Here is an instance of a suspensive conditional testamentary provision.

The testator gives and bequeaths his mansion in Lawrence, Kansas to Amanda underneath the situation that she should graduate from college. If Amanda correctly follows the condition, she will be able to receive the mansion of the testator. But if Amanda violates the state of affairs, the availability can be deemed ineffective.

The Resolutory Conditional Testamentary Provisions

In the resolutory conditional testamentary provision, the inheritance is right away transferred to the instituted inheritor upon the death of the testator. But the equal may be withdrawn from the inheritor if he does an act prohibited with the useful resource of the testator or at the equal time because the situation happens.

Below is an instance of the resolutory conditional testamentary provisions.

The testator offers and bequeaths his mansion in Lawrence, Kansas to Amanda furnished that she can be capable of not pressure below the affect of alcohol. Upon the loss of lifestyles of the testator, Amanda routinely turns into the owner of the mansion. But as soon as she is caught the usage of underneath the impact of alcohol, the mansion may be taken once more from her.

When is a state of affairs legitimate?

A testator must assign any scenario to his testamentary provision except:

1. If the scenario is against the law or morals. Conditions that require the heir to homicide a person or to steal some component an remarkable way to get his inheritance are invalid.

Conditions that save you the inheritor from fame as a witness in a case in opposition to the testator or his family are also against the law.

2. If the situation isn't always viable to do. A condition requiring the inheritor to take a step in a star is an example of an impossible situation.

The situations which is probably notable but are viable to do are legitimate. An instance of that is a situation to hike the entire Great Wall of China.

A circumstance that relies upon on the nature is likewise a valid state of affairs. A situation which incorporates,"When it rains in May, 2016"is a valid one due to the truth it's miles possible that it could rain in May, 2016.

3. If the state of affairs violate the human rights of the heirs. Conditions that prevent the inheritor to adventure, study, marry or conceive a little one are invalid situations.

An instance of this is on the same time as a husband presents a circumstance to his companion now not to agreement a next marriage after his loss of life is invalid.

four. If the scenario calls for the inheritor to execute his non-public will and institute the testator as one among his inheritor. This is known as Disposition Captatoria. This is an invalid condition as it adjustments the man or woman of wills from being gratuitous to being onerous or contractual.

To illustrate: Amanda will bequeath her vehicle to Miley if Miley also can bequeath her house to Amanda in her will.

5. If the condition offers that the heirloom shall no longer be disposed or sold by way of manner of the heir but need to be preserved to a destiny or fictitious inheritor. Since future heirs couldn't be instituted as heirs, the situation is not

feasible with the aid of the usage of purpose of regulation.

If the state of affairs is to keep the inheritance to a fictitious heir, the same is also invalid for being not possible. However, if the fictional heir happened to be just like a positive man or woman, then the condition is valid even though the testator in no manner knew the named inheritor.

For example: The testator gives her 6-karat diamond ring to John with the condition that he should maintain it until Hermione Granger arrives from Hogwarts.

This is an invalid condition because of the fact Hermione Granger defined within the will surely refers to a fictitious man or woman. But, if the testator intends to keep it to Hermione Granger best, then the scenario may be valid if someone of the same call existed at the time of the execution of the need.

What is the effect even as the situation is deemed invalid?

If the state of affairs in the testamentary provision is invalid or void, the preference does no longer grow to be null and void. The situation furnished by using the testator might be deemed unwritten. The conditional testamentary provision will then be handled as an unconditional or absolute testamentary provision.

What is the impact whilst the situation isn't always fulfilled?

If the condition isn't fulfilled, the supply and the want live valid. The belongings to take delivery of or bequeathed to the named heir will actually be once more to the property of the testator.

How must the testamentary provision be interpreted?

Testamentary provisions will be interpreted in the high-quality manner to provide effect to the want of the testator.

If the testamentary provision is capable of many interpretations, the interpretation that might offer better impact to the testamentary provision may be preferred. Another opportunity is to permit the probate or own family court docket docket to interpret the testamentary provision.

If the testamentary provision is not capable of any interpretation, the testamentary provision can be left valid but deemed not possible.

Chapter 15: Instituting an Heir

Institution of heirs is the act of the testator of naming a person or parents to inherit his belongings, rights and duties.

How can an inheritor be instituted?

The testator may moreover institute his heir or heirs thru:

Providing the inheritor's or heirs' complete names. This is the maximum strong and only way a testator may additionally institute his inheritor or heirs. There might be little room for doubt and confusion if the heirs are instituted in their entire names.

If oldsters percent the same call, then it must confer with the only defined thru the testator. If there are not any descriptions, it need to be presumed that the testator refers back to the man or woman he individually is aware of or is closest to him.

If the actual inheritor can't be established, then the organization is deemed invalid.

To illustrate:

The testator named Adam James as his heir. If there can be exceptional one Adam James, then he will become an inheritor.

If there are Adam James however one of them is the child of the testator, then within the absence of description, it is going to be presumed that he is concerning his child.

If the two Adam James are not in any manner related to the testator, none of them might be instituted as inheritor.

However, if the testator provided that his inheritor is everybody named Adam James, then each of them will inherit.

Instituting an unnamed man or woman with best descriptions. An unknown character cannot be named as an inheritor. However, if the testator supplied a specific description and one or extra person fit the outline, then the enterprise enterprise is valid.

For example:

The testator named any man or woman, who have been given a surely perfect SAT rating in 2016 but lives in Memphis, Tennessee as his inheritor or heirs. If there are 3 folks who meet the descriptions, then they all may be named as heirs. But, if no person meets the outline, the agency of heir is deemed invalid.

Instituting a alternative inheritor. A alternative inheritor or heirs are the males and females who will update the number one named heirs if they may be disqualified or couldn't be decided.

The system of instituting a replacement heir is just like instituting the number one heirs.

Instituting a fideicommissary alternative heirs. In fideicommissary substitution, the testator institute heirs. The first inheritor is charged with the obligation to preserve the all or part of the inheritance and transmit the equal to the second one heir after a specific time.

Unlike the easy substitution of heirs, the heirs in fideicommissary substitution each inherit the assets. However, the primary heir can best inherit in a restricted time.

The first inheritor is known as a fiduciary and the second one heir is the fideicommissary alternative.

To illustrate:

The testator bequeaths his assets to Henry however named him as his fiduciary heir for a length of six years. He then named Abe because of the reality the fideicommissary heir. This approach, throughout six years, Henry may be the owner of the property.

During the fiduciary term, Abe's ownership over the property is inchoate. He will incredible end up the proprietor of the assets after the quit of the term.

If within the route of the fiduciary term, the fideicommissary substitute dies, the fiduciary might be deemed as the simplest instituted heir.

Can the testator exchange his instituted heirs even after the execution of the need?

The testator can change his instituted heirs at any time after the execution of the choice with the useful resource of converting or revising his will.

Chapter 16: Disposition of the Properties with the beneficial useful resource of the Testator

What houses can the testator dispose in his will?

The testator can dispose all or any of his houses in his will. This can also additionally encompass the winning and the future homes of the testator.

However, in a few worldwide locations and states, the law limits the homes that the testator can also moreover dispose. Some prison recommendations require that the testator cannot dispose of what the regulation calls as "legitimes". Legitimes are the houses reserved via the use of the regulation to the obligatory heirs of the testator.

The regulation requiring legitimes is to defend the obligatory heirs of the testator from being left with not anything upon the lack of lifestyles of the testator.

Who are obligatory heirs?

Compulsory heirs are the humans sure thru regulation to inherit a effective part of the testator's assets. They are:

1. The youngsters of the testator;

2. The spouse of the testator;

And if the testator did now not have a partner or kids, his parents, brothers and sisters may additionally additionally moreover opportunity as obligatory heirs.

What takes vicinity if the testator did not reserve legitimes to his obligatory heirs?

If the testator failed to reserve legitimes to his compulsory heirs, the desire may be disallowed. The organization of heirs may be deemed invalid.

What if the testator left legitimes but it isn't legally sufficient for his obligatory heirs?

If the legitimes do not meet the jail limit set by manner of way of the law, the desire of the testator can nonetheless be legitimate. The stocks of the inheritor or the heirs instituted inside the will can be decreased to satisfy the desired legitime.

Are the houses obtained through way of the testator after the creation of the need nevertheless protected via the need?

Properties received thru the testator after the execution of his will may be blanketed with the aid of his will. It will be presumed that the testator possessed the houses whilst he completed the need.

What are future homes?

Future homes might also additionally moreover speak over with homes that the testator plans to build up or the homes to be obtained by using the testator after the execution of his will.

An instance of a future property is the royalties that the testator can also additionally moreover get hold of from a ebook published after his loss of lifestyles.

For example: In his will, the testator offer that his very last e-book have to be posted via taken into consideration one of his inheritor and all the royalties that he also can additionally gain from the e-book shall belong to his instituted heir.

If the ebook have come to be published and it receives a royalty of 3000 bucks for every 10,000 copies provided, the royalty shall belong to the named inheritor.

Another example of the future property is a building the testator plans to buy but the transaction have turn out to be completed after he completed the choice.

For example: In his will, James bequeathed a mansion in Chicago, Illinois to Henry. But whilst James finished the choice, he became now not yet the proprietor of the mansion. He become best planning to buy the mansion.

What if the destiny houses did not understand?

If the destiny houses did not understand or the testator did not gather the houses prior to his lack of existence, the testamentary provision will be deemed not viable.

What are inaccurate disposition of houses and what are its impact?

Erroneous disposition of houses occurs on the same time because the testator erroneously disposed a assets he did not personal.

For example: James were using the convertible BMW for a long time that he believed that he become the owner thereof. In his will, he bequeathed the auto to his chauffeur, Steve. However, upon the loss of life of James, it modified into discovered that the registered proprietor of the BMW is still his father.

Erroneous inclinations of houses are null and void.

Is the testator prohibited to promote, donate, or ruin the residences that he already disposed in his will?

The testator remains to be the proprietor of the houses that he disposed in his will. Thus, he can promote, donate or spoil the homes if he wants to achieve this. The heirs and legatees named inside the will do no longer gather any rights over the testator's houses at the identical time due to the fact the latter continues to be alive.

They can't force the testator no longer to promote, donate or damage the homes.

What takes place if the testator sells or ceased to be the owner of the houses he already disposed in his will?

If the testator bought the homes or ceased to be the owner thereof after the execution of the need, the choice remains legitimate however the testamentary provisions will not be viable.

What if the testator bequeathed his houses to 2 or greater people?

The testator can bequeath his homes to two or greater parents. If he failed to specify the stocks of every heir, the heirs are deemed to inherit the houses in identical stocks.

Chapter 17: Writing Your Own Valid Holographic Will

What are the necessities of a legitimate will?

For a will to be valid, it have to follow the intrinsic and extrinsic necessities via the regulation that operates it.

Extrinsic necessities discuss with the formalities of the want. Intrinsic requirement refers to the large factors of the want which includes the group of heirs and the testamentary provisions.

The extrinsic and intrinsic requirement of a valid will is predicated upon at the law that operates it on the time of its execution.

If the testator wrote his will in 1997 but he died in 2016, the law of succession so one can be followed is the regulation in 1997. Thus, even though the holographic will is invalid in 2016 however legitimate in

1997, the holographic will can although be allowed.

It is typically endorsed that earlier than one have to write a will, he must understand the legal guidelines and provisions of the Law of Succession that determines the validity of wills.

Extrinsic Requirements of a Holographic Will

The crucial extrinsic necessities of a valid holographic will are:

1. It should be really handwritten with the resource of the testator in a language regarded to him;

2. It should be signed and truly dated through the testator; if the will is of more than one pages, every page should be dated and signed with the aid of the usage of him as well.

If the want lacks any of those extrinsic necessities, the holographic will is deemed null and void.

Intrinsic Requirements of a Holographic Will

Most intrinsic necessities for holographic will or each extraordinary will relies upon at the legal tips of the u . S . A . Of foundation of the testator whilst the preference modified into finished. The crucial intrinsic requirement of a legitimate holographic will is that ought to be allowed thru way of the regulation that operates it. If it isn't always allowed, the whole will is deemed null and void.

But, if the holographic will is allowed, the preference may notwithstanding the fact that be legitimate but the organization of heirs and the testamentary provisions thereof may also additionally despite the fact that be declared invalid within the event that they don't observe the intrinsic requirements of the law that operates the need.

For instance: In a specific the usa, the regulation prohibits the organization of an illegitimate little one as heir or legatee in any will. Sam executed a holographic will instituting Ben, his illegitimate toddler, as his sole inheritor however introduced each other testamentary provision bequeathing fifty thousand dollars to his friend, Martin.

Though the desire did no longer have a test the operative law, the need won't be declared as null and void. Instead, first-rate the provision instituting Ben as inheritor could be declared invalid and the availability bequeathing a legacy to Martin may additionally in spite of the truth that be deemed legitimate and executory.

What regulation or laws may additionally additionally furthermore characteristic the Holographic will?

In International Law, the legal pointers which could characteristic the holographic will and all one of a kind varieties of will are:

1. The inheritance or succession law of the land wherein the want became done; and/or

2. The inheritance or succession law of america for which the testator is the citizen thereof;

The prison suggestions that feature the need need to be the felony guidelines in strain at the time even as the want became executed.

The trouble of figuring out the operative law most effective arises at the identical time because the testator achieved the choice in a rustic apart from his u.S.A. Of basis.

For example: Sam Davis, a resident of Florida executes his holographic will inside the Philippines whilst he came for a holiday. Holographic wills are legitimate in the Philippines but invalid in Florida.

Under the Philippine Laws of Succession, wills of aliens finished within the Philippines shall observe the regulation of america of a in their starting region. Sam Davis is difficulty of the Florida State succession criminal hints. Since holographic wills are not diagnosed in Florida, then the want did no longer observe the intrinsic requirement. Thus, the want and its whole provisions could be disallowed.

What are the benefit and the hazards of making a holographic will?

Many people decide upon executing a holographic will because they less complex to make and to revise. Also, it's far much less tough to keep the provisions therein secret from the heirs, for the protection of the testator and the heirs.

However, loads of world locations do not understand the holographic wills because of the hassle of authenticity. Holographic wills can with out troubles be strong by using professional forgers or falsifiers. Also, there may be no guarantee that the testator became of sound mind whilst he performed it or that he completed the want freely and voluntarily.

Another disadvantage of holographic will is that it may without problems be misplaced or destroyed. Unlike notarial wills, holographic will do no longer have any copies. Machine copied holographic wills aren't suitable. Once the particular replica is destroyed and cannot be recovered, the desire may be presumed to had been revoked.

Also, because of the fact holographic will is a mystery, it may remain as a mystery if no individual unearths it after the testator's lack of life.

How can the may be showed right?

Any person may additionally additionally moreover present a holographic will and claim that it's miles written via the deceased. Thus, in advance than the availability therein may be completely executory, it ought to be tested that all the extrinsic necessities of the holographic will are proper.